GOD
IS
GREAT,
GOD
IS
GOOD

GOD IS GREAT, GOD IS GOOD

DEVOTIONS FOR FAMILIES

BY ROLF E. AASENG

DESIGNED AND ILLUSTRATED
BY DON WALLERSTEDT

AUGSBURG PUBLISHING HOUSE
MINNEAPOLIS, MINNESOTA

To my mother
who taught me
to pray

CONTENTS

A WORD TO PARENTS

Getting to know God is an adventure in discovery—an adventure in which every member of a family can share. These devotions are intended to help families with young children on that adventure.

Because it is the source for our knowledge of God, these devotions are based on readings from the Bible. But our understanding of God takes on exciting new dimensions when we let the Bible guide us to evidences of God's activity in our daily lives, and when we share our everyday experiences with God with one another. Thus this book aims to help your family talk about your experience of God not only in the Bible but also in your lives, and to share your discoveries of God's goodness with one another.

In the first devotions we learn about God through the life of Jesus. Then we learn about him through the experiences of Bible heroes. Finally we consider how we can draw closer to God through prayer, and look at some of the things he does for us.

Each devotion's opening sentence or paragraph is intended to be used as a discussion starter before your devotional period. For example, if you have your devotions after a meal, these may give you something to talk about while eating. After the devotion has been read, the corresponding Bible verses should also be read, preferably from a modern translation. Children in the family may be encouraged to read the selections from the Bible.

The needs of your family and the setting for your devotional period will determine how you use the discussion questions, prayers, things to do, and memory verses. Other prayers may, of course, be substituted. You may wish to include a hymn as a part of your devotional period. Don't feel bound to a fixed formula. Use this book in whatever way will best help your family to discover more of the blessings God has for you.

WHAT'S GOD LIKE?

Some people think of God as an old man with a long white beard, sitting among the clouds. Some may picture him as a king on a throne. Others may think of him as a blinding light. What do you think God is like?

The truth is, nobody knows exactly what God looks like. No one has ever seen him as he really is.

In Old Testament times the Israelite people were not allowed to make any pictures or statues of God. One reason may have been that whatever they would have drawn or painted or carved would not have been nearly good enough. Also, after a time they might have started thinking that God was like whatever they had made.

Some people made figures of animals—like a calf—and said it was what God was like. But God isn't like an animal. No one can really imagine what God is like, because he is so much greater than any person.

Is there any way we can learn what God is like? There is one way. It is through Jesus. He came to tell us what God is like.

But Jesus didn't come to earth so we could learn what God *looks* like. We don't even know what Jesus looked like. We have no real pictures of him. The paintings we see are by artists who have tried to imagine how he may have looked.

Jesus came to show us the kind of person God is, not what he looks like.

If someone shows you a picture of another person, you haven't learned much about him. But if he tells you about him—that he likes to help people, that he builds cars, gives peppermints to children, and tells funny stories, you begin to get an idea of what he is like.

In the Bible, we read that Jesus helped people who came to him in trouble; that he was able to answer the hardest questions; that he was stronger than storms and sickness and even death. As we learn what Jesus is like we learn about God, for Jesus is God's son.

When you wonder, "What is God like?" think of Jesus. For Jesus is like God.

Bible reading: John 1:18

Why didn't God want the Israelites to try to make pictures of him? Where do we get our ideas of what Jesus looked like? What are some of the things you have learned about God by learning about Jesus?

Father, we thank you that we can get an idea of what you are like by learning about Jesus. We're glad that you are what you are. Amen.

Something to do:

See how many pictures of Jesus you can find. Display the one you like best on your bulletin board or in your room.

13

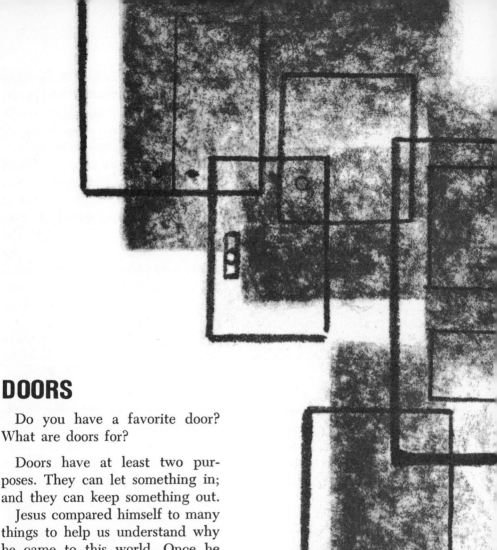

DOORS

Do you have a favorite door? What are doors for?

Doors have at least two purposes. They can let something in; and they can keep something out.

Jesus compared himself to many things to help us understand why he came to this world. Once he called himself a door. That means he opens the way for us. Jesus says that if we come in by him (in other words, if we follow him), he will care for us.

He will be a door to let us in to God's family where we can be close to him forever. He will show us how God loves us and what he is

tear us away from God. As long as we believe in Jesus and let him be the door that brings us into God's treasure house, he is also like a door closed tight to keep evil away.

We act as doors too. Sometimes we slam shut at the wrong time. By being rude or mean; by refusing to help others; by being selfish; by forgetting what God would like us to do, we are like locked doors that keep some people from good things that God wants to give them through us. Instead, we keep them out where they can be hurt.

But we can be open doors too. Jesus will help us. As we help other people and tell them of God's love, we are opening doors to let people come in to get the good things God has for them.

Bible reading: John 10:7-10

To what does Jesus let us in? What does Jesus keep out? How can we be doors?

Thank you, Jesus, for being a door for us so we can receive all the good things you have for us. Help us to be doors so others can have your blessings too. Amen.

Something to do:

Think of ways you can be a "door" for at least one person by tomorrow—then do it.

doing for us every day. He will tell us how to be happy and how we can help others. He will forgive us when we do wrong. Maybe you can think of other things Jesus does for us.

Jesus says there is no other way to receive these good things he has for us. Jesus is the only way—the only door to what God has to give us.

But Jesus says that he is also a door to keep something out. After we come into his house, he shuts out things that would harm us. He keeps out thieves and robbers—the devil and others who would cause us trouble, make us unhappy, or

15

OUT OF THE DARK

Which do you like better, light or darkness? Why?

If you have ever been afraid in a dark place, you will especially like one of the names Jesus gave himself. "I am the light of the world," he said.

The Bible often speaks of God as being a light. When the people of Israel were crossing the desert, God sent them a large flame at night to let them know he was with them and to show them the way to go. At Pentecost, God put flames of light on the heads of those who believed in Jesus to show he was sending them the Holy Spirit.

We are hardly ever in a completely dark place, with no street or yard lights, no headlights, no flashlights, no moon or stars. If you have ever been in a deep cave when the guide turned off all the lights for a few seconds, you know

what it is to be in the dark. We can't live that way, without light.

Jesus is light. That is another way of saying he shows the way.

If we walk in the dark, we can get into all kinds of trouble. We won't know where we are going and may end up where we don't want to be. We have to move slowly, and even then we are sure to stumble over anything in our way.

If we try to live without Jesus it's like walking in the dark: We're

16

not sure where we'll end up and we'll stumble into trouble. But if we listen to what Jesus tells us, he will be a light to show us the way to live now, and finally the way to heaven.

Some light is reflected. The moon, for example, reflects the light of the sun. When we keep in touch with Jesus, we begin to reflect his light. When we do things for others, they may see God's light reflected in us, and their lives will be helped. Jesus gives us his light so we can help him be a light for the whole world.

None of us wants to live in the dark all the time. Jesus came to bring light to our lives and to the lives of all people.

Bible reading: John 8:12

Why is light important? What does it mean that Jesus is a light for our lives? What may be some of the results in our life if Jesus is our light?

Thank you, Jesus, for coming to be our light. Help us to follow you closely so you can give us the light we need for our lives. Amen.

A verse to remember:

"I am the light of the world; he who follows me will not walk in darkness" (John 8:12).

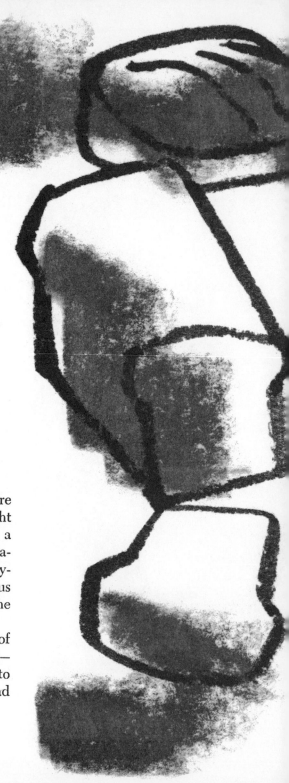

BREAD

How important is bread?

If you were going to compare yourself to something, you might pick an animal (like a tiger), or a plant or tree, or maybe even a machine. But can you imagine anyone calling himself bread? Jesus did. "I am the bread of life," he said.

Often when the Bible speaks of bread it means all kinds of food—everything we need from day to day. By calling himself bread

the ground and ate it. Without this bread they would have starved.

Jesus is as important to us as manna was to the Israelites in the desert—as important as food is to keep us alive today.

Jesus, our bread, not only makes us to be alive. He gives us a life that is interesting and good for something, one that is useful.

Sometimes Jesus called the life he gives eternal life. This eternal life begins for us now as members of God's family. It means we shall always be with God, and that's when life is the happiest for us.

Jesus is the bread of life for us because he takes care of us better than anything we can find in this world.

Bible reading: John 6:29-35

Why is bread (or food) important to us? Why did Jesus compare himself to bread? Name at least one good thing about the life Jesus gives us.

Lord Jesus, we thank you for your promise to give us a wonderful life. Help us to live for you and to serve you always. Amen.

Something to do:

Look for a picture of sheep and a shepherd or of Jesus the Good Shepherd and bring it to your next family devotion.

Jesus was telling his followers how important he is to us.

He was probably thinking of the strange kind of bread God provided for the Israelites when they lived in the desert as they made their way from Egypt to the land God had promised them. They called this bread manna. Every morning the people picked it from

WHO NEEDS
A SHEPHERD?

Look at a picture of a shepherd. Have you ever seen a shepherd? What does he do?

Most of us don't know any sheep. Mary with her little lamb doesn't go to our schools. We may have seen sheep on a farm or in a zoo, but most of us have not watched sheep enough to see how they behave. And we know very little of how a shepherd takes care of his sheep.

Jesus called himself the Good Shepherd. What does a good shepherd do? Jesus says that he gives his life for his sheep. That hardly seems possible, does it? A flock of sheep is peaceful and quiet—not dangerous at all.

20

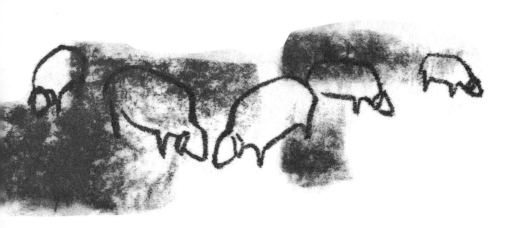

But life isn't always so quiet for shepherds. King David, as a young man, had to fight lions and bears while he took care of his father's sheep. He was a good shepherd because he was ready to risk his life for the sheep.

Jesus is that kind of good shepherd for us. He left heaven to live a hard life on earth for us. He came to earth because he cares for us and for all people. He was willing to risk his life for us. As a good shepherd he died for us on a cross.

Jesus is not only *a* good shepherd—one of many. He is *the* Good Shepherd—the best one, the only one. He gave his life to care for us, so that we could belong to him. Besides that, he takes care of us, as a shepherd cares for sheep. The sheep depend on their shepherd for food, for shelter in bad weather, and for protection against enemies. Jesus, the Good Shepherd, does all these things for us too.

To know that Jesus loves us so much that he gave his life to keep us safe is the best thing to know in the whole world.

Bible reading: John 10:1-11

What does a good shepherd do? How is Jesus like a shepherd? Who is like a shepherd for us today?

Thank you, Jesus, for taking care of us, and for giving your life for us. Amen.

Something to do:

Find a vine or a branch and bring it to your next family devotion.

21

BRANCHES

Take a look at a branch or a vine. Where did it come from? What does a branch do?

How many apples or cherries would you get if you cut a branch off a tree while it was still full of blossoms and stuck it into the ground?

You would soon have nothing but a dead stick. We know that if a branch is going to grow and produce fruit, it has to be connected to roots that can send food up the tree trunk to the branches. If it is cut off from the tree, its leaves and blossoms will soon dry up and drop off.

Jesus said that it is just as important for us to be attached to him as it is for a branch to be connected to the trunk of a tree. "I am the vine," Jesus said; "you are the branches."

He was talking about grape vines, because many of the people he was talking to grew grapes. But the same thing could be said of any tree with branches. Unless we are connected to Jesus we will become like dried up branches.

But if we stay with him, we live and do good things. Jesus calls this "bearing fruit." It's natural, just as

it is natural for a healthy apple tree to bear good apples.

We bear fruit when we do for others what Jesus himself would do: when we help people, forgive them if they do something against us, and show by our actions how much God loves us all.

When we act in this way, says Jesus, we show that we are his disciples—that we are connected to him as branches are connected to a vine.

And if we act in this way, we shall be glorifying our Father in heaven. In other words, we'll be telling the world how great we think God is.

Bible reading: John 15:1-8

Why is it important for a branch to be connected to a vine or tree? How can we be connected to Jesus? What happens when we are connected to Jesus?

Thank you for all you have done for us, Jesus. Help us always to depend on you as a branch depends on a tree, so we may keep doing more for others. Amen.

A verse to remember:

"I am the vine, you are the branches. He who abides in me, and I in him, he it is that bears much fruit" (John 15:5).

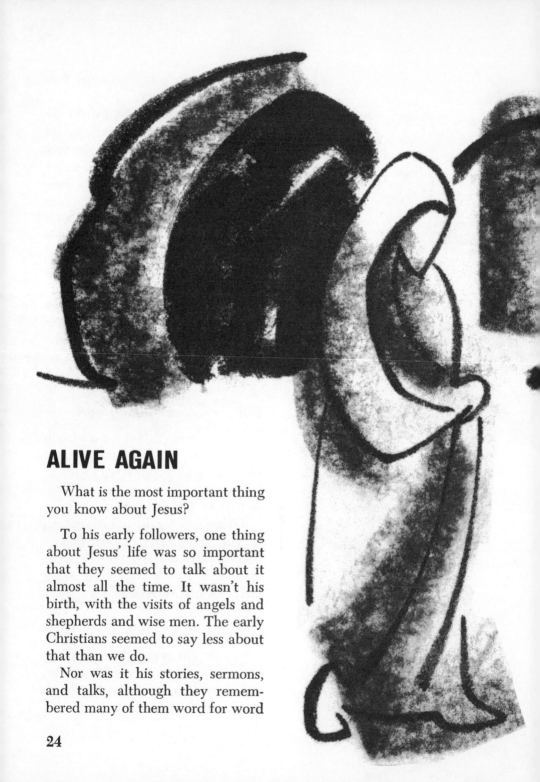

ALIVE AGAIN

What is the most important thing you know about Jesus?

To his early followers, one thing about Jesus' life was so important that they seemed to talk about it almost all the time. It wasn't his birth, with the visits of angels and shepherds and wise men. The early Christians seemed to say less about that than we do.

Nor was it his stories, sermons, and talks, although they remembered many of them word for word and told them often to one another and to others.

It wasn't the miracles he did, showing his love for people in need and his power over everything in the world as he stopped storms, healed sick people, and even made dead people alive.

What the first Christians talked about most of all was how Jesus became alive again after he had died. As far as they were concerned, the most important thing about Jesus was his coming back to life.

Jesus talked about it too. "I am the resurrection and the life," he said to a friend named Martha. She was very sad because her brother Lazarus had died.

Martha was sad especially because she knew Jesus could heal sick people. She said to him, "If only you had been here earlier my brother wouldn't have died."

But Jesus had something to teach her. He told her not to stop hoping for good things to come, because he was resurrection and life. "Whoever believes in me," he said, "even though he dies, yet he shall live."

Martha couldn't understand what he meant. Even when Jesus brought Lazarus back to life she may not have known what he was telling her.

We can understand better what Jesus meant. We know that he died and came to life again and that he will bring us all to life again after we die. If we believe in him, we have hope even if someone close to us dies.

We don't get very old before we know that all people die. It makes us sad. But Jesus is stronger than death. He is life, he said; he is resurrection. And he promises that when we believe in him we don't have to worry about dying. He will raise us to a new life.

Bible reading: John 11:21-27

Why was Martha sad? What is there about Jesus that can make us less sad when someone dies? Why is it important for us that Jesus came alive again after he died?

Lord Jesus, we thank and praise you that you came to life again after dying. Help us to depend on your power to overcome our fear of death. Amen.

Something to do:

If you know someone who has lost a friend in death recently, send him a card expressing your sympathy and faith.

LITTLE PEOPLE

Have you ever gone to a church service where people acted as though you weren't there?

Sometimes ushers at church may not bother to say "Good morning" to children. Or they may forget to give them bulletins or hymnals. It is almost as though they can't see anyone smaller than 40 inches high.

On the other hand, some grown-ups pay too much attention to children in church. Has anyone ever turned around and looked at you in a way that seemed to say, "What are you doing here anyway?"

You can be sure if Jesus were here children wouldn't be overlooked. Once some mothers brought their children to see Jesus. He was busy, as always, answering questions and healing sick people. When the disciples saw the mothers trying to push their way through the crowd to bring their children to Jesus, they tried to send them away. "Jesus is too busy to bother with kids now," they told them. "Don't disturb him."

But Jesus didn't agree. He was busy, but not too busy for children to see him. "Let the children come to me," he said; "don't keep them away."

Then he said something more—and it sounds strange at first. "Heaven belongs to children and to those who are like children," he said. He probably meant that even grownups are like children compared to God. Only those who recognize how much greater God is than we are, and are willing to accept what he gives us—as a child accepts a gift—will come into God's kingdom.

Jesus always has time for children, just as he has time for all kinds of people. Some people may push you aside and think you're too little or too young or not very important. But Jesus thinks you are important. You are important enough for him to come to this world to be your Savior. He always has time to listen to what you want to tell him and to help you. He wants you to be in his kingdom with him.

Bible reading: Mark 10:13-16

Why did the disciples try to keep the children from Jesus? Why does Jesus want children to come to him?

We thank you, Jesus, that you want little people in your kingdom. Help us to love those who don't feel important enough to come to you. Amen.

Something to do:

Think of ways children can get more good out of attending church, and then use those ways next Sunday.

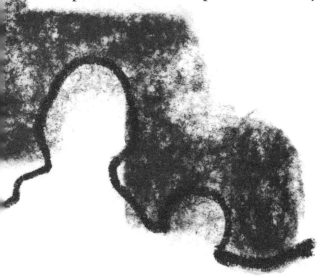

LOST AND FOUND

Have you ever lost something that you liked very much? How did you feel?

Someone once asked a woman who had many children, "Which one of your children do you love the most?" She answered, "The one who needs love the most." If one of her children was hurt, or sick, or had a problem, that was the one she loved in a special way.

God is like that. Some people said evil things about Jesus because he spent so much time with bad people. His answer was that he came to help those who needed help. God loves all his children; but he tries the hardest to do something for those who are in greatest need.

Jesus once told a story to help people see why he felt as he did. "If you have 100 sheep," he said, "and one of them is lost, what do you do? Don't you leave the 99 that are not lost and go to look for the one that is missing?

away from him or need his help. When one of those people is finally reached so God can help him and bring him back into his family, there is a real celebration in heaven.

Sometimes we forget those who are lost from God's family. We may try to have nothing to do with those who are different from us, or who do things we don't like. But God loves them—all of them. He is always trying to help them.

He wants us to help them too. No one is so good that he doesn't need God's help. And no one is so bad that God doesn't love him and try to help him. When we remember how good God has been to us, we will want to be helpful to others.

Bible reading: Luke 15:1-7

Why did Jesus spend time with people who weren't very nice? How should we act toward those who don't belong to a church, and may not even want to belong?

Thank you, Father, for giving us help. Give us more of your love so we can help more people. Amen.

A verse to remember:

"The Son of man came to seek and to save the lost" (Luke 19:10).

"You climb down steep and rocky cliffs. You go where wild animals live. When you finally find the lost sheep, you carry it home, and you let everybody know how happy you are. You may even ask your neighbors to help you celebrate."

In the same way, said Jesus, God loves those who have wandered

OUT OF THE TREETOP

If Jesus were speaking somewhere today, to how much trouble would you go to hear him?

The people of the Holy Land where Jesus lived were curious to see and hear him. Often they would travel a long way or go to a lot of bother to be near him.

One day Jesus was going through a town called Jericho. As usual, many people wanted to see him; they crowded around the road he was traveling, just as though there were a parade.

In the crowd was a very short man named Zacchaeus. He found taller people in front of him wherever he tried to get a look at Jesus. Maybe they stood in front of him on purpose, because Zacchaeus wasn't very well liked.

But Zacchaeus didn't give up. He figured out where Jesus would go next, then ran ahead and climbed up into a tree by the road. From there he could have a good look at Jesus when he passed.

He got more than he was looking for. When Jesus came near the tree, he stopped, looked up, and spoke to him. "Zacchaeus," he said, calling him by name. "Hurry up and come down. I would like to have dinner at your house today."

Zacchaeus was so surprised he hardly knew what to say. But he quickly climbed down from the tree and gladly took Jesus to his home. Now he could not only look at Jesus but he could talk to him too.

He learned to love Jesus and decided that very day to live the kind of life Jesus would want him to live.

Jesus was ready to be the friend and Savior of a man no one else liked. He is our friend and Savior, too, and because we know him we

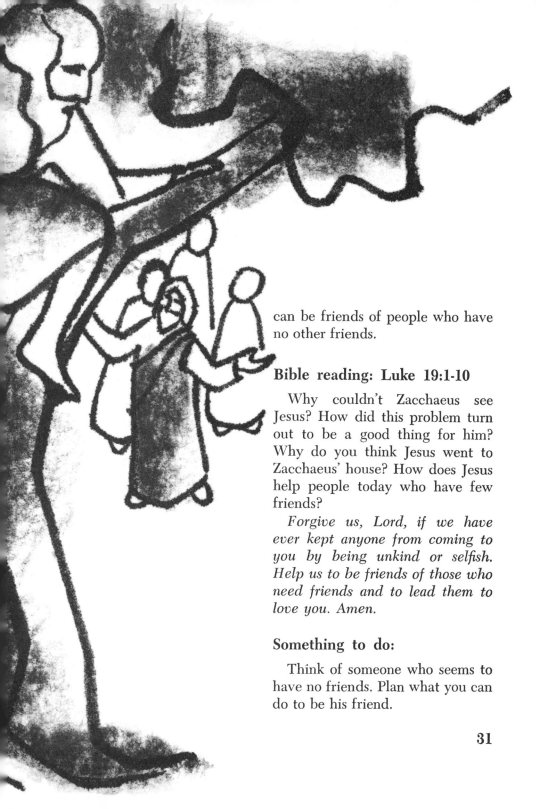

can be friends of people who have no other friends.

Bible reading: Luke 19:1-10

Why couldn't Zacchaeus see Jesus? How did this problem turn out to be a good thing for him? Why do you think Jesus went to Zacchaeus' house? How does Jesus help people today who have few friends?

Forgive us, Lord, if we have ever kept anyone from coming to you by being unkind or selfish. Help us to be friends of those who need friends and to lead them to love you. Amen.

Something to do:

Think of someone who seems to have no friends. Plan what you can do to be his friend.

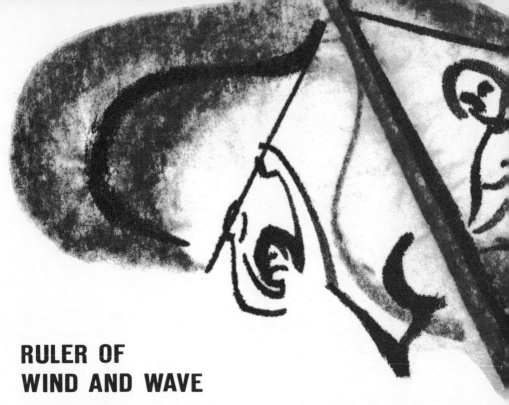

RULER OF
WIND AND WAVE

Some people like storms. Others are very much afraid of them. You may have a cat or dog that hides under the bed during a thunderstorm.

Once a bad storm really scared the disciples of Jesus. They were crossing a large lake in a small fishing boat when suddenly a windstorm struck. The waves dashed higher and higher, and their boat was being tossed about like a small piece of wood.

Jesus was with the disciples in the boat, but he was tired and had fallen asleep. Even the storm didn't wake him. The disciples fran-tically tried to bail water out of the boat and to keep it headed into the waves so it would not sink. But as the storm got worse they became afraid they weren't going to make it, so they woke Jesus, saying, "Save us, Lord, we're sinking."

Jesus acted as though they shouldn't have been afraid of anything as long as he was with them. "Why are you afraid?" he asked. Then he told the storm to stop—and it did.

The disciples had seen Jesus do many miracles before, but they were amazed by this. What kind

of person was Jesus, they wondered, that even the wind and waves would obey him when he spoke to them.

Later they learned what we know, that Jesus was not only a man, but that he is God too. That's why he had power over storms. And because he was God the disciples didn't have to be afraid in the storm when he was along.

The disciples learned to depend on Jesus to take care of them when they were in trouble. We can depend on him too. We know that Jesus is stronger than anything in the world. We can be sure that he is able and willing to help us too when we're in danger.

Bible reading: Matthew 8:23-27

What scared the disciples? Why didn't they need to be afraid? How could Jesus have so much power? How might he help us in danger?

We too are amazed when we think of your power, Jesus, and even more when we think of the fact that you use that power to help us. We look to you for protection against the storms of life that might hurt us. Amen.

Something to do:

Talk about how you might get over being afraid of something.

TWO ROLLS AND SOME SARDINES

If your family is like most, you probably go on picnics in the summer time. What kind of picnic do you enjoy most?

People have always enjoyed packing a lunch and eating out of doors. Even in the Bible there are stories that remind us of picnics.

Once Jesus went with his disciples into the country, far away from any towns, for a vacation. But many people who liked to listen to him found out where he had gone and followed him. Among them was a boy who may have decided to make a picnic out of it: he took along a lunch.

Although Jesus wanted a rest, he talked to those who came flocking after him because he knew they needed his help. They were so interested in what he had to say that they stayed way past meal-time. The disciples realized that it was getting late, and they tried to get Jesus to send the people home to eat.

But Jesus surprised them by suggesting that they should treat the crowd to a meal. That meant they would have to feed about 5,000 men, and women and children besides.

Where could the disciples get enough food for all these people?

There were no stores nearby, and even if there had been, they didn't have enough money to buy food for everyone.

Then one of the disciples discovered the boy who had brought his lunch. All he had was two small loaves of bread and five fish —probably about as much as a few rolls and a can of sardines.

But he let Jesus have what he had. And because he did, Jesus in a wonderful way used that small amount of food to feed all those people.

That's the sort of thing that can happen when we let Jesus have full use of whatever we have, whether we have much or little.

Bible reading: Mark 6:31-44

Why was food needed? Who supplied the food? Why do you think Jesus did this miracle?

We have food and other things, Lord, which many people do not have. Help us to see how we can best let you use what we have to help others. Amen.

Something to do:

Plan to do something to help feed people who are hungry. As an example, you might eat nothing but soup or oatmeal for one meal and give the money you save to a relief organization.

35

HEROES

Who do you think are the three or four greatest or most important people who ever lived? Why?

None of us will ever be able to say "thank you" to all the people who have done something for us. We don't even know who they all are. Many of them lived long before we were born. Hundreds, perhaps thousands of individuals have done things that make our lives easier and happier.

This is especially true when it comes to our faith in God. We are helped to understand God and worship him not only by the life of Jesus, but also by what many people learned and did long ago.

The writer of the Letter to the Hebrews names several heroes of faith. Many of the names are quite familiar to us: Abraham, Joseph, Moses, David, Samuel. Others are less familiar, like Abel, Gideon, or Samson. And there are some that

we may not even remember hearing about, such as Enoch, Barak, and Jephthah.

But they are all heroes of faith—along with thousands of others whose names may not be written down anywhere. They did great things for God because they loved and trusted him. Their lives have helped many people.

Some of them won great victories over evil. They won battles; they escaped danger; they helped others. On the other hand, some, instead of winning, got into much trouble because they believed in

God. They were thrown into prison or were beaten or even killed.

But they all kept trusting and obeying God. Many of them probably didn't think they had done anything great and would be surprised that we call them heroes.

The stories about these heroes of faith can encourage us to do what God wants us to do. We can ask God to make us brave and wise enough so that someone who lives after us will find it easier to love God because of what we have done.

Bible reading:
Hebrews 11:32—12:2

Who are some of your favorite heroes of faith? What did they do? What good does it do for us to remember these people?

We thank you, God, for people whose faith has helped us to believe in you. We are thinking of some of them now. Help us to be faithful to you as they were. Amen.

Something to do:

Make a list of people from long ago and today who have helped you.

WITHOUT
A ROAD MAP

Some families like to go on long trips. What is the longest trip you've ever taken?

Try to imagine what it would be like to take a long trip if you didn't have a car, or if there were no trains or airplanes to carry you. Suppose you had to walk all the way, or ride horseback. And suppose there were no paved roads— only dusty trails—and no road maps. And what if you knew that there wouldn't be any hotels or motels where you were going, and no relatives to visit—no one that you knew. In fact, the people probably wouldn't want you to be there.

This was the kind of trip Abraham had to make. God asked him to leave his home town, not just to take a trip or make a visit, but to move his home hundreds of miles away. He didn't even tell Abraham where he was to go; he just said, "Go to a place that I will show you."

Yet Abraham trusted God enough so that he was willing to start out. Because of this, something wonderful happened—something good for Abraham and for the whole world, even for us. For the place to which God led Abraham is what we sometimes call the Holy Land, because that is where Jesus lived many years later. There

dreds of years later something good happened for all of us.

Sometimes God may want us to do some scary things. We won't always know how it is going to turn out. But we can be sure, as Abraham was, that whatever God wants us to do is right. And it will lead to blessings of many kinds for us and for others.

Bible reading: Genesis 12:1-7

Who told Abraham to move? Where was he told to go? What good things happened because he went? What do you think God would like you to do now that might be hard to do?

Help us, Lord Jesus, to understand what you want us to do today, and make us willing to do it. Amen.

Something to do:

Find a story in a book or magazine about someone who did something brave to serve God.

Abraham settled down, and his family grew into the nation called the Israelites.

Because he believed God, Abraham was blessed—good things happened to him. Not only did he become a famous man in his new homeland, but he was an ancestor of Jesus, who blesses us all. Because Abraham obeyed God, hun-

A LONG LADDER

Sometimes when we travel in a strange part of the country, or when we move to a new place to live, we can feel very much alone. If your family has ever moved, you may have had this lonesome feeling.

When Jacob had to leave his home to live in a different country (because he had cheated his brother and was afraid of him), he must have felt very lonely and afraid. One night as he was traveling, he camped out in a field. While he slept he had a strange dream. It helped him to get over that feeling of being all alone.

Jacob dreamed that he saw a ladder reaching up to heaven from the spot where he was sleeping. Angels were going up and down the ladder. At the top was God, who told Jacob that he would always be with him, no matter where he went.

Maybe Jacob didn't know before he had that dream that God can be everywhere. Maybe he thought God had left him because he had done some bad things. At any rate, this dream taught him something about God and his love for us. Although he had troubles later on, Jacob always remem-

40

bered this dream and the promises God gave him.

We can be as sure as Jacob that God is always with us, because God makes the same promises to us. Jesus himself said, "I am with you always."

So if you have to move to a strange town or country, or if you ever travel somewhere far from home, or if you have to leave friends behind, you can always be sure that God is with you, no matter where you go. You don't have to feel alone or scared.

God is always near enough to hear our prayers. And wherever we go there will be someone near who loves God and will be a friend to us.

Bible reading: Genesis 28:10-17

What did God tell Jacob in a dream? What has Jesus promised us? How can you help someone who is a stranger or is lonely to know that God is near?

We thank you, Lord, that you are always near. Help us never to feel afraid or lonely. Amen.

A verse to remember:

"I am with you and will keep you wherever you go" (Genesis 28:15).

41

IN JAIL

Do you think God would ever want a person to be in prison? How could someone serve God in prison?

Joseph must have wondered how he could do anything for God where he was—in jail. The worst thing about it was that he hadn't done anything wrong. He was in jail because someone told a lie about him.

But Joseph didn't give up or get angry with God. He tried to do what he thought God would like him to do, even in prison. He was helpful and honest. The keeper of the prison noticed this. He gave Joseph jobs that gave him some freedom inside the prison. In this way Joseph met people who later would be able to help him get out of jail.

One of these was a man who had a strange dream. God helped Joseph to explain what the dream meant. Later the man got out of prison and went to work for Pha-

raoh, the king of Egypt. He promised to try to help Joseph get out of jail. But no sooner was he free than he forgot all about Joseph.

A few years later Pharaoh had a strange dream. Then the man finally remembered Joseph. He told

This made it possible for Joseph to help his father Jacob and his brothers, along with many other people, when they had nothing to eat.

It took many years before God's plan for Joseph finally worked out. In spite of many troubles, Joseph didn't give up his trust in God. Because of that God was able to use him for a very important job that helped a whole nation.

We won't all be as famous as Joseph. Most of us aren't likely to have as much trouble as Joseph either. But we can learn from him to keep on believing in God, whether we have troubles or not. We can be sure of God's promises to take care of us. And sooner or later he can bring about something good.

Bible reading: Genesis 39:19-23

How did Joseph act in prison? How did the trouble that came to Joseph turn into something good? Can you think of some trouble that came to you or someone else and later turned out good?

Father, help us to keep believing that you will keep your promises and bring us through whatever troubles may come to us. Amen.

Something to do:

Make a list of some of the promises God has given us.

Pharaoh that he knew a man in prison who could explain dreams. The king sent for Joseph at once.

Again God helped Joseph to explain the dream. The king was so pleased that he gave Joseph an important position in the government.

EXCUSES
THAT DIDN'T EXCUSE

Have you ever been asked to do
something you were afraid to do?
What did you do about it?

First Moses was curious. Then he
was surprised. Then he got scared.

While he was herding sheep
Moses saw a bush on fire. Although
it kept burning, it never seemed
to burn up. Moses walked over to
get a better look, and suddenly a
voice called his name.

"I am God," the voice said. This
must have been more than enough
to make Moses nervous. But when
he heard what God had to tell him,
he really got scared.

God wanted Moses to go back to
Egypt. Years before, Moses had
run away from that country because he had committed a crime
and the police were after him. To
go back would be dangerous.

God also wanted him to tell
Pharaoh, the king, to let the Israelite people leave the country.
Even if Pharaoh didn't know that
Moses had run away, Moses knew
that he would not be pleased with
anyone who suggested the Israelites should leave. They did much
work for the Egyptian government.

But God had a job that needed to be done and he wanted Moses to do it. He promised to help. He made Moses able to do miracles, and he found someone to make speeches for him. Moses finally agreed to do what God asked. As a result, the Israelites were able to leave Egypt for a country where they could be free.

God may not have as great a work for us as he had for Moses. But what he wants us to do may still take courage. He may ask us to say something for him to people who won't like it any more than Pharaoh. But he promises to help us, as he helped Moses. We will never know what he can do through us unless we listen when he has something to say to us.

Bible reading: Exodus 3:6-12

What did God want Moses to do? Why didn't Moses want to do it? How was he finally able to do the job?

Father in heaven, forgive us for sometimes not wanting to do what you ask. Help us to believe that you can do great things for us. Amen.

Something to do:

Think of one job that God wants you to do and begin doing it.

No wonder Moses began thinking up all kinds of excuses for not doing what God wanted. "I'm not the man for the job," he said. "Nobody knows me. Even the Israelites won't listen to me, much less Pharaoh. No one will believe that God has talked to me. And I can't even give speeches."

THEY SPIED ON GIANTS

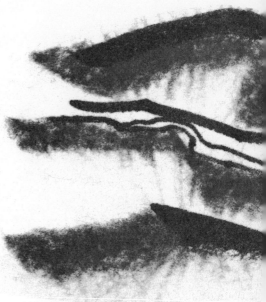

Can you think of a time when you or someone else became unpopular because you did what was right?

Caleb and Joshua weren't very popular with the Israelites. They said something the people didn't want to hear. No one agreed with them. It wasn't a good feeling at all.

Moses had sent them and ten other men to find out what Canaan was like. This was the land God promised to the Israelites. They were to learn all about it before the Israelites tried to move in and live there.

When they came back the spies reported that it was a very good land. The Israelites would be able to grow enough of everything they needed. But, the men said, some fierce people lived there. Some of the spies even called them giants.

And ten of the men said, "We'll never be able to get any land for ourselves; these people will drive us out." They persuaded the rest of the Israelites that instead of going to the land God wanted them to have, they should go back to Egypt, to be slaves for Pharaoh again.

Only Caleb and Joshua objected. The people in the new country were strong, they agreed. But they remembered how God had led them out of Egypt when it seemed impossible. "If we go back now," Caleb and Joshua said, "We shall be disobeying God. God is with us; we don't have to be afraid."

The people wouldn't listen. They would have killed Caleb and Joshua if God hadn't stopped them. They didn't believe that God could or would do what he had promised.

God didn't let them go back to Egypt. But because the Israelites wouldn't do what he commanded, they did not get to the land he had promised them until about 40 years later. None of those who were so

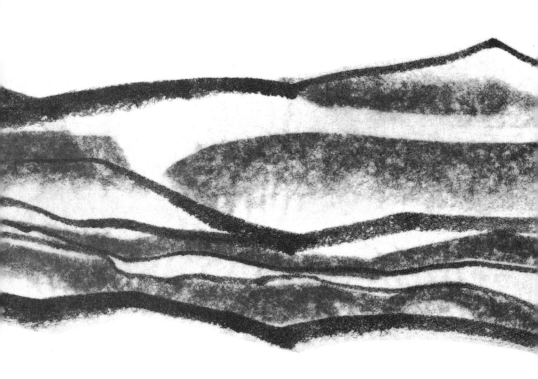

afraid to do what God wanted even got into the new land. They had to live the rest of their lives in the desert. Only Caleb and Joshua lived long enough to move into the land they were sure God would give them.

Bible reading:
Numbers 13:25-32

How were Caleb and Joshua different from the rest of the spies? Whom did the people believe? What happened to Caleb and Joshua? What can you do if you are alone in standing up for what is right?

Help us not to be afraid of what others may think of us, God, but to stand up for what we know is right even if no one else will. Amen.

Something to do:

Make a list of people who stood up for what they believed was right even though others made fun of them. Try to find and read a story about one of them.

TOO MANY SOLDIERS

Someone once said, "One with God is a majority." Was he right?

Can you imagine anyone saying in the middle of a war: "We have too many soldiers. Send most of them home"?

When the Israelites were trying to gain their freedom from an army that had invaded the country God had given to them, God told their general, Gideon, "You have too many soldiers. Let anyone go home who wants to."

When Gideon announced this, most of the soldiers were only too glad to go home. Hardly anyone likes to fight in a war.

But 10,000 men were left, ready to go into battle for their country.

God said, "That's still too many." He told Gideon to use an unusual test to pick out those who should stay. "Send your soldiers down to the river for a drink of water," he said. "Pick out those who take some water in their hand up to their mouths. Send the rest of them home —those who put their heads down to the water."

Gideon used this test and ended up with only 300 soldiers. And he was supposed to lead them against an army of thousands!

But that was just enough for God. He wanted the Israelites to understand that he was going to win the victory for them. They couldn't do it by themselves no

matter how many soldiers they had. But with God the number of soldiers really wasn't important. He was the one who made the difference.

In the middle of the night the 300 soldiers who were left surrounded the enemy camp. Instead of spears or swords each one carried a trumpet and a jar with a torch in it. When Gideon gave a signal they all blew their trumpets, broke their jars, held their lighted torches high, and shouted.

The enemy soldiers woke up, heard the noise, and saw the lights all around the camp. They thought they were being attacked by a huge army, so they ran away, and the Israelites were free. And they knew that God had done it for them.

Bible reading:
Judges 7:2-8, 19-23

Why did God want the Israelites to have a small army? How did they win the battle? Can you think of a time when God did something for someone that seemed impossible?

We need your help, God, to win the battles against evil in our life. Help us to listen to your word and depend on your leading. Amen.

A verse to remember:

"With God nothing will be impossible" (Luke 1:37).

A VOICE IN THE NIGHT

Does God ever talk to you? How can you tell if it's God?

Samuel was a young boy when God first spoke to him. For a while he didn't know who was talking to him.

Samuel had gone to live with Eli, the priest, at the house of the Lord. It was like a school away from home for him. Eli taught Samuel many things about God. In addition, Samuel ran errands for Eli.

One night after Samuel had gone to bed, he heard someone call his name. Supposing that Eli had another job for him to do, he ran to the priest's room to see what he wanted. Eli was surprised to see him. "I didn't call you," he said.

Samuel returned to his room, probably wondering if he had dreamed that he heard a voice. But before long the voice called again, "Samuel." Samuel was sure he wasn't dreaming this time, so he went to Eli again and said, "Here I am. What do you want?"

Again Eli said, "I didn't call you Go lie down again."

Samuel must have wondered if someone was playing a trick on him. He was probably still trying to figure it out when the voice

heard his name to say, "Speak, Lord, I'm listening."

Samuel went back to his bed. Imagine how excited he must have been, wondering whether it really was God, and hoping that he would speak again.

Sure enough, the voice called again: "Samuel, Samuel!" Samuel answered in the words Eli had told him to use. Then God spoke again and gave him a message for Eli.

Many times throughout his life Samuel heard God speaking to him, and he was careful to listen and obey. This made him a great ruler.

We aren't likely to hear a voice calling our name, as he did. But God speaks to us too—through the Bible, through the words of people who believe in him, through our thoughts. If we listen, he will tell us what we need to know.

Bible reading: 1 Samuel 3:2-10

Why did God call to Samuel? What can you do when you think God is speaking to you?

We thank you that you speak to us, Lord. Help us to recognize your voice and to listen to what you have to tell us. Amen.

Something to do:

Make a list of things God has told you lately.

called to him a third time. Samuel didn't know who else would be calling his name at that time of night, so he went back to Eli. Eli realized that it must be God who was calling Samuel. He told him to lie down again, and the next time he

A SECRET SIGNAL

Who is your best friend? Why? What makes a friend?

David and Jonathan had worked out a secret code to send messages to one another. They were best friends. That was surprising. For Jonathan was the son of King Saul. And it was natural in those days for the son of the king to become king after his father.

But Jonathan knew there was a good chance that he wouldn't become king after his father—because of David. David had been chosen by the prophet Samuel to be king. Most of the people liked David; they didn't care that he wasn't Saul's son. It would have been natural for Jonathan to be jealous of David, and even to do anything he could to keep David from being king.

But Jonathan wasn't like that. He was David's friend. He was even ready to help him be king.

His father, King Saul, didn't like David. When he learned that Jonathan and David were friends he became angry.

Jonathan knew what true friendship is. He risked his life to warn David that his father was trying

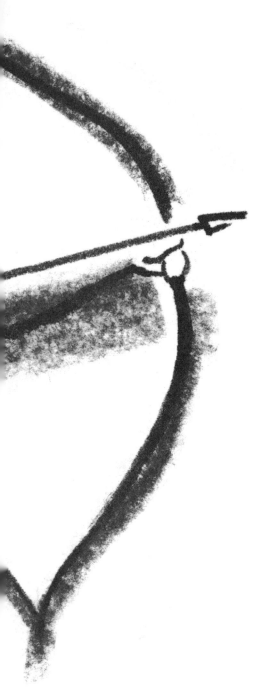

to kill him. That's when they made use of their secret code. They worked out a signal so Jonathan could let David know what he should do so Saul wouldn't catch him.

Jonathan took a bow and arrows into a field where David could see him from his hiding place. Jonathan purposely shot an arrow beyond the servant who was supposed to pick it up. This was to let David know that he had to run away and hide.

Jonathan was eager to help his friend David, even if it cost him something. That's the kind of friend Jesus is to us. He wants to help us, even though it cost him something to come to earth to be our Savior.

Bible reading: 1 Samuel 20:1-9

Why was it strange that David and Jonathan were good friends? How did Jonathan show his friendship? How can you show your friendship to others?

Thank you, Jesus, for being my friend. Help me to be a true friend to others. Amen.

A verse to remember:

"Greater love has no man than this, that a man lay down his life for his friends" (John 15:13).

HE STOLE A SPEAR

Right or wrong: If someone has done wrong to us, and we have a chance, we should pay him back.

David had helped King Saul in many ways. Yet Saul tried several times to kill David. He was jealous because people talked about all David had done, even more than they talked about Saul's deeds. As a result, David often had to leave his home and hide.

54

Once Saul went with his soldiers to try to capture David. They camped near a place where they knew David was.

During the night David and one of his soldiers sneaked into Saul's camp. They got right up to Saul's tent and found him sleeping, with his spear stuck into the ground close to his head.

The soldier who was with David said, "Here's your chance. God has put Saul into your hands. I can kill him before anyone even knows we're here, and he won't bother you any more."

It would have saved David a lot of trouble. And it might have saved the nation of Israel trouble too because Saul was not a very good king. But David said, "No, don't hurt Saul. God made him king; let God take him away if he wants to."

So they left the camp. But they took along Saul's spear. When they were a safe distance away, David shouted to the commander of Saul's soldiers and told him he was a poor watchman. He showed Saul the spear he had taken to prove that he wasn't going to harm the king even if he had the chance.

Saul was ashamed when he realized how unfair he had been to David. And for a time he stopped trying to capture David.

Often we want to get even with a person who has done something wrong to us. If someone hits us we always want to hit him back. But that usually causes even more trouble.

The Bible says that getting even is God's job. He will take care of anyone who harms us.

Bible reading: 1 Samuel 26:6-12

Why might David have wanted to kill Saul? Why didn't he do it? What should we do when someone is always bothering us?

When people do wrong to us, Lord, help us to trust you to take care of them in the best way. Give us your love so we can be kind to them. Amen.

A verse to remember:

"Vengeance is mine; I will repay, says, the Lord" (Romans 12:19).

ONE WISH

If you were told that you could make one wish for anything you wanted, what would you ask for?

Solomon had just become king after his father David when God appeared to him in a dream and asked him, "What would you like me to give you?"

Many things must have crowded into the mind of the new king. He would have found many ways to spend millions of dollars. He might have wished that he could win a great battle, or that he might have a strong group of helpers to stand behind him. Then he would have felt much safer as king.

He might have asked for a beautiful wife; or a long, peaceful reign as king. He might even have wished to get revenge on the people who had tried to keep him from becoming king.

But Solomon decided to ask for none of these things. He thought about the important job he had been given, to be king over the Israelites. So he told God, "I need help in doing my job. Help me to understand what is right and what is wrong so I can govern the people in the best way possible."

God was pleased with this request. He not only gave Solomon what he asked, but he also gave him many other things. He made him rich. During his reign Israel was at peace with other countries.

But above all God gave Solomon the ability to know what is right.

in the New Testament, "If any of you lacks wisdom, let him ask God —and it will be given him."

Bible reading: 1 Kings 3:5-13

What did God tell Solomon in a dream? What did Solomon ask for? Why? What was the result? How can we become wise?

Thank you, God, for giving us what we need. Help us to know the things that are most important and to ask for them. Amen.

Something to do:

Read some of the Proverbs (which were written by Solomon) to see what advice you can find that can help you today.

He made him wise—so much so that people came from far away countries to listen to Solomon. He is still known as the wisest man who ever lived.

Perhaps James was thinking of Solomon and how God had answered his prayer when he wrote

57

ONE AGAINST 450

Try to imagine what it would be like if yours were the only family in town that believed in God and everyone else had a different religion.

It would be one against 450. There was only one prophet of the true God. His name was Elijah. But 450 priests served the idol called Baal. Yet Elijah challenged them to see whose God was the strongest. The priests of Baal agreed to a contest; after all, there were so many more of them. They shouldn't have any trouble winning.

Each side would build an altar and on it put an animal to be burned as a sacrifice. They were to get everything ready except for one thing: they wouldn't start the fire. Instead, they would ask their god to send fire. And the one who started a fire would be accepted as the true God.

The prophets of Baal tried first. They built an altar out of stones. On it they put wood to burn, and a bull. They then began to call on Baal to send fire. But nothing happened.

They kept on asking for hours—all morning long. They shouted and jumped up and down. They even cut themselves with knives to see if their god would notice them then. Elijah made fun of them—which sounds like a dangerous thing to do. "Call louder," he said. "Maybe your god is away on a trip, or maybe he is sleeping."

But nothing happened.

Finally they gave up. It was Elijah's turn. He put wood and an animal on his altar. Then he did a strange thing. He poured on pails of water until water was standing on the ground around the altar. Finally he prayed: "O Lord," he said, "show these people that you are God."

Right away fire came down. It not only burned up the wood and the sacrifice, but even the water on the ground and the stones in the altar.

When the people saw that, they all said, "The Lord is God." They admitted that an idol has no power and that they had been wrong to worship anything but the true God.

Bible reading: 1 Kings 18:30-39

How was Elijah going to show who was God? How did the test turn out? How can we today show people that our God is the true God?

We thank you, Lord, that you are the God of all, and that you use your power to work for us. Help us to live in such a way that people will know that we serve you, the true God. Amen.

A verse to remember:

"The Lord, he is God" (1 Kings 18:39).

SEVEN SNEEZES

What happens to people when they die?

Ordinarily we don't pay much attention when someone sneezes. A sneeze isn't anything unusual, nor do we think of it as a happy sound. But long ago when a boy sneezed, not just once, but seven times, he caused a great deal of excitement. Those near him prob-

ably thought it was the best sound they had ever heard.

This boy had just died. He was a very special boy. He had been born as a gift of God to an old couple who had no children. God had given them this child in their old age because they had been kind to Elisha, one of the greatest of the Old Testament prophets.

too. So he prayed to God and held the boy next to himself. Then the boy sneezed seven times, and Elisha knew that God had made him alive again. He called to the mother and gave her back her son, perfectly well.

It is unusual for God to bring back to life someone who has died. The Bible tells us of only a few times that Jesus did it. But these few times remind us that God has the power over life for all people. He gave us life once and he can do it again. And because Jesus rose from being dead he has told us that at the end of the world he will bring us all to life again to live with him forever. That is something to look forward to and to thank God for.

Bible reading: 2 Kings 4:32-37

Why was the boy a special boy? Who caused the boy to live again? What has God promised us after we die? What difference does that promise make to our life now?

Father, we thank you that you have power over life and death. Amen.

A verse to remember:

"I am the resurrection and the life" (John 11:25).

You can imagine how happy they must have been when after years of waiting they had a baby. How thankful they were to God! No wonder they were really upset when a few years later the boy died.

The mother went at once to find Elisha. He came back with her and found the boy dead. It upset him

61

THE LOST BIBLE

What would you do if suddenly there were no Bibles anywhere? Would it make any difference to you?

In our country it's hard to imagine a time or place where there would not be even a single Bible. It was different hundreds of years ago. Then all books had to be copied by hand, one by one. There were no libraries or bookstores, and buildings weren't the best for keeping things dry and clean. There were few books of any kind.

Still, you'd think that a book as important as the Bible would surely be kept in a safe place. Yet there was a time in the kingdom of Judah when no one knew where to find a copy of the book that would be like our Bible. In fact, no one even seemed to know there was such a book.

King Josiah had ordered some men to repair the temple. The carpenters working there found a book and gave it to the priests. They found that it was the book

had not been doing what God had told them in the book.

So Josiah commanded all the people to come to listen while he read to them from God's book. Then he announced that he was going to worship the true God as the book said he should. The people said they would worship God too. Because of what he did as he tried to obey God, Josiah is remembered as one of the best kings of Judea.

We may not have to worry about losing all Bibles. But sometimes they might as well be lost for all we use them. God has given us the Bible so we can know him as a loving Father. King Josiah read and believed what God had to tell him and received the blessings God wanted him to have.

Bible reading: 2 Kings 22:8-13

What did King Josiah do when he found the book of God? How should we use God's book? How can we be sure we won't ever be without God's Word?

We thank you, God, that we have the Bible. Help us to read it, believe it, and obey it. Amen.

Something to do:

See how many Bibles you have in your house. Find out when and where you got them. See if you can tell how they are different.

of God's law. It may have been misplaced years before when the rulers of the country didn't believe in God. Or it may have been hidden by someone so it wouldn't be destroyed. The priests brought the book to King Josiah.

When the king heard what was in the book he became very upset. He realized that he and the people

HE SAID NO
TO THE KING

Can you think of any time when you would have to be different from most people around you if you were to do what God wants?

Daniel was a lucky boy—in some ways. To be sure, he had been taken captive with other Israelites by the Chaldeans. But at least he wasn't killed. Instead, he was picked to go to school in the palace.

Daniel soon discovered that some of the things he was expected to do, even some of the food he was given to eat, were against the rules God had given his people. He wondered what he should do. He knew the king wouldn't be very happy if anyone—especially a prisoner of war—said that the food in the palace wasn't good enough for him.

Should he do what the king commanded, even though he knew it wasn't right? He could always excuse himself by saying that they might kill him if he didn't do exactly as they said.

But Daniel would not go against God. If he was sure that God wanted him to do something, he did it—no matter what might happen to him. So he asked the man in charge of his class if he could have some different food.

The man liked Daniel, but this request worried him. He was afraid he would be killed if he didn't train the boys just as he was told.

Daniel suggested to the man who served the meals, "Let's try eating the kind of food that God has told our people to eat. If we start losing weight or get weak, then we'll eat what you want." The man agreed to try this as an experiment for ten

days. Daniel expected that God's way would prove to be the best.

At the end of ten days, Daniel and his friends who joined him in refusing to eat the king's food were healthier than others in the class. So they were allowed to continue eating the food that was permitted according to their religion. At the end of their training they were given important jobs where they could serve God and their people.

Daniel dared to do what he was sure God wanted him to do, even though his actions might have caused him trouble.

Bible reading: Daniel 1:8-16

What didn't Daniel want to do? Why? Why was it dangerous for him to refuse to do this? Can you think of times when God would want you to dare to be different?

Forgive us for so often being afraid to do anything that other people will think strange, even if we know it's right. Help us to do what we know is right at all times and depend on you to take care of us. Amen.

Something to do:

See if you can find a story about someone who stood up for what he believed even if it was dangerous for him.

THE LIONS KEPT THEIR MOUTHS SHUT

What would you do if there was a law that no one was allowed to pray, even at home, and anyone caught praying would be punished?

The king had taken a liking to Daniel. This made some other men jealous. They tried to catch Daniel doing something wrong so they could tell the king about it and get rid of Daniel. But Daniel kept God's laws so well that they could find nothing to complain about.

The men learned, however, that Daniel's faith meant more to him than anything. They decided to trap Daniel. They knew that he always prayed three times a day, at the same time.

So they tricked the king into signing a law which said that for 30 days no one was allowed to pray to anyone except to the king himself. If anyone did, he would be thrown into a den of hungry lions. The king must have been a very proud and foolish man to agree to such a law, but he did.

The men who had made the law went to see if they could catch Daniel praying. They found him praying in front of his window. Daniel was more interested in pleasing God than anything else. So they arrested him. The king realized then that he had been tricked but it was too late. The punishment had to be carried out. All the king could do was pray that Daniel's God would save him.

He prayed all night. Early in the morning he ran to the hole where the lions were and shouted, "Daniel, has your God saved you from the lions?"

To the king's great relief, Daniel answered, "My God sent an angel and shut the lions' mouths; they haven't hurt me."

Maybe that's what Daniel expected. Or maybe he thought he would be killed. He knew that it was important for him to be true to God. He left it up to God to save him if that was what he wanted.

We aren't likely in our days to be thrown to lions for praying. But there may come times when we may get into trouble if we put obedience to God above everything. Whether we suffer for it or not, we can be sure that God will take care of us in the way that is best.

Bible reading: Daniel 6:10-22

Why did the men get the strange law passed? What kept the lions from harming Daniel? Will God always keep us from harm as he kept Daniel?

Help us to trust in you as Daniel did, O God, so that we shall always be more concerned to do your will than about what happens to us. Amen.

A verse to remember:

"He is able to do far more abundantly than all we ask or think" (Eph. 3:20).

67

LOOK, GOD

Where is God now?

Some people seem to think that God lives in church buildings, and that he doesn't often go out. Others seem to think that God is far away in heaven.

God is present in church buildings, to be sure, and he is also in heaven. But that's not all. He is also right here with us, wherever we are. When he left his disciples to return to heaven, Jesus promised, "I am with you always."

In Old Testament days it may have been easier, at least for some people, to understand that God is near us. God had a way of letting the Israelites know he was around. An unusual cloud near their camp during the day, and a big flame of fire at night, told the people God was there.

68

all the time, seeing what they do and hearing everything they say. They have the idea that God is watching them to see if he can catch them doing something wrong —and that if he does, he will punish them.

God doesn't want us to think of him in that way. He tells us through his Word that he is a loving and gracious God who cares for his people. And he is with us all the time, to help us.

When one little girl heard about God being with her all the time, she thought it was great. She clapped her hands and said, "Look at me, God, I'm jumping rope."

After they built the tabernacle —a tent that served as their church building — the cloud or the fire stayed right over it. In this way God wanted to show the people that he was there among them.

We don't have anything like a cloud or fire to tell when God is with us now. But we can depend on his promise that he is here.

Some people feel uneasy when they think of God being near them

Bible reading: Exodus 40:34-38

How did the Israelites know God was near? How do we know he is near? How does it make you feel to know God is near?

Thank you, God, for being near us all the time. Fill us with your joy. Amen.

A verse to remember:

"Lo, I am with you always" (Matthew 28:20).

WHAT TO SAY

Whom do you like to talk to most? Why?

We don't have any trouble talking to our friends. No one has to tell us what to say to them. We don't even find it hard to talk to them when we can't see them, as when we talk over the telephone.

But sometimes we may find it harder to talk to Jesus. Maybe it is because we know he is so much greater than we are. Most of us are shy when we are near any great person. We don't know what to say. We're happy if he does most of the talking.

Maybe it is hard to talk with Jesus because we have never seen him. We may wonder just what he is like and what he would want us to say to him.

It doesn't have to be harder to talk to Jesus than it is to speak with our best friend. We don't need a special language. We can use our own words and talk the way we usually talk. We don't have to use any special words. Jesus wants us to talk to him the way we really think and feel.

When we are going to talk with Jesus it is a good idea to let him say something first. This means we need to read the Bible, in which Jesus speaks to us. There we learn what he is like so we can feel more comfortable talking with him. We find that he is a kind person, interested in all that we do, who wants to help us just as he helped people in Bible times. He promises to give us what we ask for. And he tells us what he has already done for us when he came to the earth to be our Savior.

All this helps us know what to say. We can talk to him as a friend who understands us. Probably the

first thing we want to say after learning about Jesus is "Thank you." We can thank him for life; for food; for all God has given us; and for making it possible for us to be with him in heaven.

Bible reading: John 15:7-16

What kind of words should we use in praying? How can Jesus talk to us? What do you think is most important to say to him?

We thank you, Lord Jesus, that we can talk with you in prayer. We thank you that you are interested in us and want the best for us. Help us to be thankful for what you do for us. Amen.

Something to do:

Find a prayer or a hymn that says thank you to God.

BEFORE THE PILGRIMS

What things are you most thankful for?

When we think of thanking God, we may remember the Pilgrims who came to America long ago. They set aside a day of thanksgiving because they were thankful to God for letting them live in a new land. But this wasn't the first Thanksgiving Day.

Long before the Pilgrims, even before Jesus lived on earth, the Israelite people used to gather together to thank God for his goodness. These were special days, something like our Thanksgiving. At one of them (called the feast of harvest or weeks) they brought a gift of two loaves of bread made from wheat they had just harvested. By this gift they were telling everyone that they knew God was

the one who made their crops grow. They were saying "Thank you" to him. Until they had brought this gift they wouldn't eat anything they had grown.

Later in the fall they had another celebration, which lasted a whole week. It was called the feast of tabernacles. At that time they came together again to thank God for everything that had grown in their fields, such as raisins, figs, olives, and grain. Again they gave gifts to God from these crops.

This was a happy time. The people sang songs thanking God, and played musical instruments, too. God had been very good to them, they all agreed.

Not many of us grow our own food. But we still know that everything we have comes from God. So Christians, like the Pilgrims and the Israelites of long ago, like to gather together to thank God for what he has done.

Bible reading: Psalm 100

Why did the Israelites bring two loaves of bread to their church? What are some of the things you are most thankful for?

Thank you, God, for giving us all the things we need to live, and for caring for us day by day. Amen.

A verse to remember:

"Enter his gates with thanksgiving, and his courts with praise" (Psalm 100:4).

HARD WORDS

Have you said "Thank you" to anyone today?

Some mothers and fathers believe that the hardest words for their children to learn to say are "Thank you." How many times has it happened in your family that someone has received a gift, and mother or father has had to remind, "What do you say?"

Some of the people who received things from Jesus found it hard to say thank you. Once as Jesus was entering a town, ten men who had leprosy called to him from a distance, "Jesus, Master, have mercy on us." They wanted him to cure them from their sickness.

Jesus didn't say he would heal them. He just told them to have a priest look at them. In those days the priests often took the place of doctors; they had to decide if people were really healed from a sickness.

The men must have believed that Jesus would heal them because they started off to find a priest. As they went, they noticed the

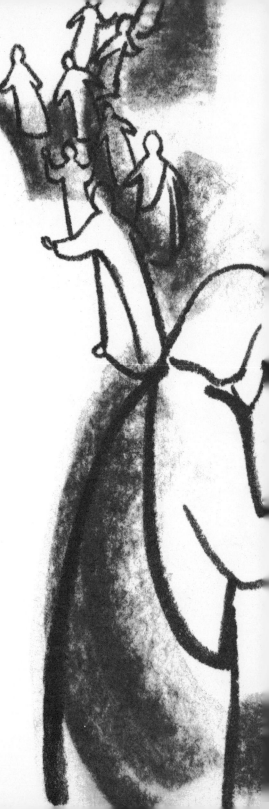

74

sores on their skin disappearing. They were suddenly well!

One of the men, when he saw this, turned around right away and ran back to Jesus to thank him. The others kept on going.

Jesus sadly asked, "Didn't I heal all ten? Aren't any of the rest even going to say 'Thank you'?" But Jesus was happy that at least this one man had come back to thank him.

Bible reading: Luke 17:11-19

What did Jesus do for the ten men? Why do you think nine of them didn't say "Thank you"? Try to think of a time when someone thanked you. How did it make you feel?

Thank you, Father, for being patient with us when we forget to say "Thank you." Help us to remember to say "Thank you" to you and to others. Amen.

Something to do:

For the next day make a special effort to say "Thank you" every time someone does something for you.

WHAT COMES AFTER THANK YOU?

What do you think Jesus would like us to talk about with him?

When we talk to a person, no matter how much he has done for us, we don't just keep on saying to him, "Thank you, thank you, thank you." Nor does Jesus want us to say only thank you prayers. He invites us to talk about many things.

recitation of special words we have learned in church. But this isn't natural. Jesus is our friend, and we can talk to him about anything in our own words.

When we remember how powerful Jesus is and how much he cares for us, we soon think of something to ask him. We might ask him to help us choose friends or TV programs, or how to spend our money.

We might ask him for things we need: health, money for certain things, jobs, help to understand our lessons.

We might ask him to forgive our mistakes—those we couldn't help, and those we could have.

We might ask him for help to be more kind to others, more loyal to our church and our friends, to be a stronger follower of his.

We might ask for anything we need. Jesus is ready to hear us.

Bible reading: John 14:12—13

What can we talk to Jesus about in prayer? What might we ask for?

Help us to think of the best things to ask you for, Lord Jesus, and help us also to use well the gifts you give in answer to our prayers. Amen.

Something to do:

Find a hymn or prayer, or make one up, that asks for something in a way you like.

We can tell him what we are doing, how we feel, what troubles we have or the mistakes we make, what we plan to do, what we are wondering or worrying about, or what makes us happy. We may talk to him about anything.

This may not sound like prayer. But sometimes we make prayer too hard. We may think it is only a

77

PROMISES

How many promises about prayer can you think of from the Bible?

If you ask your parents for a sandwich, will they give you a stone, maybe one that looks like a piece of bread? Or if you ask for a piece of fish to eat, will they hand you a poisonous snake? Of course not, says Jesus. What kind of parent would do that?

Most parents try to give their children the things they need, especially things as necessary as food or clothes. If for some reason they can't give what is needed, they surely won't try to fool a child with something else, or give something that would be harmful.

If we can expect parents to give children what they ask for, said Jesus, surely we can expect God to give his children the things they need. For God is much greater than the best parents.

God is always fair and helpful. He is so powerful he can do anything. If parents give good things

to their children, how much more will our loving Father in heaven do the same.

God wants us to talk with him in prayer and to ask him for what we need. More than that, he promises that he will answer our prayers. The promises God has given us in the Bible are the basis for all Christian praying.

His promises sound a little hard to believe—until we remember how much God has to give, and how much he loves us. We remember also how much he has already given us: our lives, and all that keeps us going. And above all, the gift of Jesus our Savior.

Sometimes we may ask for something that would be harmful for us or someone else. A good parent won't give what we ask for then, nor will God. But he has promised that he will give good things to those who ask. And he waits for us to ask.

Bible reading: Matthew 7:7-11

Why do we pray? For what can we pray? What can we do if God doesn't give us what we ask for?

Thank you, Father, for promising to hear and answer our prayers. Amen.

A verse to remember:

"Ask, and it will be given you; seek, and you will find; knock, and it will be opened to you" (Matthew 7:7).

DON'T LEARN IT TOO WELL

What is the first prayer you ever learned? Who taught you to say it?

If you have always been used to saying prayers, it may seem strange that some people don't know how to pray. But when you stop to think about it, everybody has to be taught how to pray. If this doesn't happen when we are small, we may

not know how to go about it when we are older.

Even people who began to pray when they were very small may have to learn how to pray again when they are older. Maybe the only prayers they learned were some rhymes they repeated before they went to sleep, or before eating. They may have learned them so well that after awhile they didn't even have to think about what they were saying. They just said the first word and their mouth took over.

That isn't praying; that isn't talking to anyone. It is only repeating words.

All of us need to learn new ways to pray as we grow older, just as we learn to do other things better as we grow. We have new ways of thinking about things and new problems to pray about.

The disciples often heard Jesus pray. After hearing him, they knew they had more to learn about prayer. So they asked Jesus to teach them.

We still use the answer Jesus gave them as a prayer. We call it the Lord's Prayer. It includes the main things that a person who believes in God is concerned about. Jesus didn't mean that we should use only the words he spoke when we pray. But we can use his prayer as a pattern for other prayers that we make up by ourselves.

Is it possible to learn the Lord's Prayer too well? Sometimes we rattle off the words so fast, without thinking, that it doesn't mean anything to us. That doesn't show much respect for the person we're talking to—and it isn't prayer.

If we use the words Jesus taught his disciples as a guide for our prayers, and as we read other things Jesus said about prayer in the Bible, we can learn how to pray better. And we shall find that prayer becomes more interesting and brings us closer to God and his will all the time.

Bible reading: Luke 11:1-4

Why do people have to be taught to pray? How can you learn to pray better?

Father, teach us to pray. Amen.

Something to do:

Find and learn a new table prayer—or make up one of your own.

HE'S WAITING

Would you think of calling God "Father" if Jesus had not told us to do so?

Jesus called God "Father" and he asks us to do the same. A good father will often act toward his children as God acts toward us, but no father on earth comes anywhere near being the kind of Father God is.

Some of the parables Jesus told help us to understand the kind of Father God is for us. One of the most famous of these stories is the parable of the prodigal son.

A son demanded that his father give him some money. Then he went as far away from his home as he could go. He wasted all his money on foolish and sinful things until he had nothing left. He couldn't even get enough to eat.

He thought of his home and decided that it hadn't been such a bad place after all. He knew that because of the way he had acted toward his father he didn't deserve to be in the family any more. But if he went back maybe his father would hire him as a servant.

Then at least he would get enough to eat.

That's the part of the story we may remember best. But the important part comes next. The father had been waiting, all the time the son was gone, for him to come back. He must have known the son had wasted his money and had done many wrong things. Yet, he even used to go out and look down

82

God is like the father in this story. He has many reasons to be angry with us because of the way we have wasted what he has given us and done wrong. But he loves us so much that when even the worst of us begins to think of changing his ways, God is there waiting to welcome us back.

No matter how we may have disobeyed him or disgraced his name, God is always waiting for us to come back and be in his home forever.

Bible reading: Luke 15:11-24

Why might the father not have welcomed the son back? Why did the father welcome him? Why does God welcome sinners back? What does it mean to you when you call God your Father?

We thank you, our Father in heaven, that we can call you our Father, and we thank you for being the kind of Father you are. Amen.

A verse to remember:

"As a father pities his children, so the Lord pities those who fear him" (Psalm 103:13).

the road, hoping to see his son coming.

One day he saw him. He ran down the road to meet his son. Before anything was said, he welcomed him with a kiss. He didn't even let his son explain that he wanted a job as a servant. Instead the father started getting ready to have a party to celebrate, he was so glad to have the son back.

TAKE OFF YOUR SHOES

Has your mother ever told you to take off your shoes? Maybe after you walked in the mud on a rainy day?

Moses was once told to take off his shoes. It wasn't because he might track in mud on a newly washed floor. And it wasn't his mother who told him to take off his shoes. It was God. What difference did it make to God whether Moses wore shoes?

This happened when Moses was taking care of sheep. He saw a burning bush on the mountainside. When Moses went over to take a closer look, God told him to take off his shoes.

God caused the bush to burn to get Moses' attention. He had a job for him to do, and some things to teach him. One of the things he wanted Moses to learn is that God is holy. So when Moses came near, God said, "Take off your shoes—you are standing on holy ground."

The place was holy because God was there. Any place where God is present is holy, because God is

84

holy. That means that he never does anything wrong; that he always does exactly what he should. It means that he is perfect. He is without sin. It means that he is different from all people in the world, because all of us sin.

Ordinarily something or someone that is holy can't stand to be near anything that isn't holy. But the amazing thing about God's holiness is that even though God is holy and we aren't, he wants us to come to him, just as he wanted Moses to come to the burning bush.

All he asks is that we "take off our shoes"—in other words, get rid of any idea that we are as good or as holy as God is. He wants us to come to hear what he has to tell us. And he promises that he will take away the sin that keeps us from him. He will make us holy, too, so we can live with him.

Bible reading: Exodus 3:1-6

Why did God want to get Moses' attention? Why did God tell him to take off his shoes? How can we "take off our shoes" before God?

Forgive us for not respecting you as a holy God. Forgive our sin and make us holy. Amen.

Something to do:

Bring a seed to your next family devotion.

LIKE A SEED

Look at a seed. How big will this seed grow? Are there other seeds that grow larger? What makes them grow?

Many seeds are so small that you can hardly see them—especially if they are lying in the soil. Not until they begin to grow do you even know that they are there. But after they begin to grow, they can increase their size thousands of times. Sometimes a very small seed grows into a large bush or tree, even breaking apart rocks with its roots as it grows. It may become big enough to hold birds or animals— even people. Great power is packed into a seed.

Jesus said the kingdom of heaven —the place where God rules—is like a seed. What God does when he begins to work in a person or a community may seem to be very little. Many people don't even notice that anything is happening. But once God's kingdom gets a foothold and starts to grow, nothing can stop it.

God promises that when his word is proclaimed, something will happen. It begins when someone reads the Bible or hears about the goodness of God. Like a seed, God's kingdom will start to grow in that person's mind. And once it begins growing, nothing can stop it, except the person himself, for God's power is at work. It will change people; it will defeat evil and bring happiness.

No matter how many people in the world don't even see it, or consider it too little to pay attention to, God's kingdom is here. And he will cause it to grow and carry out his good purposes in our lives and in the world.

Bible reading: Matthew 13:31—32

How is God's kingdom like a seed? How can we help God's kingdom grow among us?

Show us how we can help your kingdom to grow, God. Amen.

Something to do:

See if you can find a plant that has grown up to show its power by cracking a rock or concrete.

GOD CHOSE THE BRIDE

How does God let us know what he wants us to do?

Abraham had given his servant a hard job. He told him to go back to the country they had moved away from and find a wife for his son Isaac. In those days the parents chose the person their son or daughter would marry. Abraham wanted to be sure Isaac married someone who believed in God, and the people in his new homeland didn't believe.

The servant wondered how he could be sure he would choose the right woman for Isaac's wife. He decided he needed God's help.

He travelled until he came to a well outside the village where Abraham's relatives lived. There he waited, for he knew that soon young women would come out to the well to get water. As he waited he prayed that God would show him the girl to pick. He asked that this girl would not only offer him a drink of water but would also offer to get water for his camels. He knew that anyone who would do that would be kind and generous and a willing worker.

Before he had ended his prayer a girl came to the well. He asked

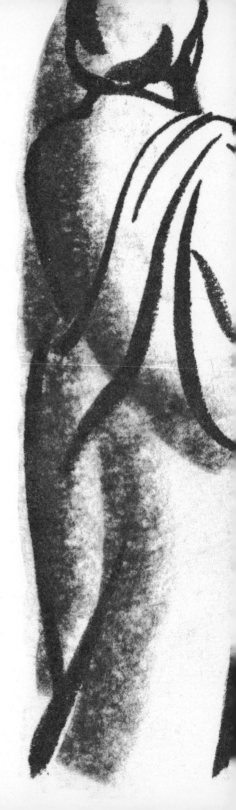

her for a drink of water and she quickly gave him one. Then she said, "I will get water for your camels too." The servant was surprised that God should answer his prayer so quickly. He at once thanked God for leading him to the girl.

The girl, whose name was Re-bekah, told her family what had happened at the well. They invited Abraham's servant to stay at their house.

He told them how Abraham had sent him to find a wife for Isaac.

He said he had asked God to show him whom he should pick, and that Rebekah seemed to be the answer to his prayer.

When the family heard what he said, they agreed that it was God's will that Rebekah should be Isaac's wife, and they let her go back with Abraham's servant. Isaac married Rebekah and they lived together many years.

Bible reading: Genesis 24:12-21

What did the servant do to make sure he would get the right wife for Isaac? How can we learn what God wants us to do?

Lord, we want whatever you want to happen, because we know that is best. Help us to know your will for us. Amen.

A verse to remember:

"He who does the will of God abides forever" (1 John 2:17).

WHAT IS IT?

Do you remember what manna was?

You've seen dew on the ground. What if one morning, instead of dew, you should see the ground covered with some kind of small flakes? You'd probably say, "What is it?"

That is exactly what the Israelites said. They had been complaining to Moses because they did not have enough to eat. God told them that they would have bread the very next day.

In the morning they saw this strange stuff on the ground. It looked like frost; but it wasn't cold enough for that. So they said, "What is it?"

Moses told them, "It is the bread God promised you." Since it was something new and didn't have a name they called it manna—which is what their first words, "What is it?" sound like in the Hebrew language.

The Israelites had a chance to learn better than anyone else how God provides what we need to live. If God had not sent the manna they would have had nothing to eat. At other times he supplied water and gave them meat by sending flocks of birds.

God had another lesson for them. If they tried to keep some of the manna until the next day, it spoiled. God had promised to send the manna each day. He wanted to show that they could depend on him always to do what he promised.

God no longer feeds us with miracle dew, as he did the Israelites.

But he still supplies what we need to eat. Many people work to produce and prepare the food we buy at a grocery store. But all still comes from God, for without the rain and sun he gives so plants and animals can grow, there would be nothing to eat.

Now we try to have more than one day's supply of food on hand, but we still pray for daily bread. By that we are saying that we know all our food, and everything else we need, comes from God. And we ask for it one day at a time because we can be sure that God will take care of each day as it comes along.

Bible reading: Exodus 16:13-18

What was manna? How does God provide our food? Why do we pray for daily bread?

For giving us food every day, we thank you, God. Amen.

Something to do:

Try to find out where the food you had today came from. How many people helped to prepare it for your use?

$10,000,0[0]

A 10 MILLION DOLLAR GIFT

How much is what God does for you worth?

Ten million dollars! Most of us have a hard time even trying to imagine how much money that is, or how much it would buy, or how big a room it would fill. We know that it's far more than we or our parents are likely to earn in a whole lifetime.

Jesus told a story about one man who owed someone 10 million dollars. How could he ever pay back so much money? No matter how hard or how long he worked, he could never pay the debt.

To have the man to whom he owed all this money say, "That's all right; you don't have to pay it back"—that was almost unbelievable! He could hardly be given a greater gift.

The story gives us a hint of how much God has done for us. We can't measure it in money, of course; no one could figure out in

dollars and cents what God has done for each of us. He has given us our life—our homes and country —our abilities to do different things. He has invited us into his family to be with him forever. Because of Christ's love for us he forgives us for what we do wrong.

If we tried to put a price on all of that, we know it would be a huge amount. It would be more impossible to pay God back for all he has done for us than it would be for us to repay someone 10 million dollars. No amount of trying to be good, no amount of going to church and Sunday school or keeping rules, would add up to much compared to what God has done for us.

But God tells us: "No matter how much you've done wrong, I forgive you. All these things that will help to make your life happier I want to give to you. You don't have to try to pay me back for any of it. I am doing this because I love you."

That's better than a 10 million dollar gift!

Jesus goes on to say that after all we have received from God, the least we can do is to forgive others. We forgive other people because we know how often God forgives us.

That thought is a part of the prayer Jesus taught his disciples. We still pray, "Forgive us our sins as we forgive those who sin against us."

Bible reading: Matthew 18:23-35

Do you think it is right to compare what we have received from God to 10 million dollars? What can we do to show how thankful we are for what God has done for us? What makes us willing to forgive those who do something against us?

Thank you, Father, for forgiving all our sins. Help us to forgive others as we have been forgiven. Amen.

A verse to remember:

"I will forgive their iniquity, and I will remember their sin no more" (Jeremiah 31:34).

FIRST CHOICE

Who is the most generous person you know?

Some wise mothers, when they have to divide a piece of pie between two children, tell one child to divide it in two pieces. They then give the other child first choice. You can be sure that the two pieces are divided as equally as possible.

Most of us try to get the biggest and best of something we like for ourselves if we have the chance. That can lead to trouble, for us and for others.

When God told Abraham to move to a new country, his nephew Lot went with him. They lived so close together that their cattle and sheep were often on the same pasture. Before long the hired men began quarreling, trying to get the best grazing land and water holes for their own animals. Abraham and Lot agreed to move farther apart.

Abraham could have ordered Lot to go somewhere else. God had given this land to him. Instead, he generously told Lot to pick out the land he would like to have, and he would give it to him. Lot chose what looked like the best land. If Abraham was foolish enough to give it to him, he probably told himself, why not?

Abraham did not become poor because he gave Lot first choice. God was more than able to take care of his needs. People don't often lose because they are generous.

But Lot probably lived to be sorry he had been selfish. His greed landed him in a place where he was often tempted to do wrong. He came to live in the wicked city of Sodom, which God later destroyed. Lot barely escaped with his life, let alone his money. Because he put himself first he got into trouble.

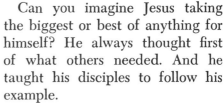

Can you imagine Jesus taking the biggest or best of anything for himself? He always thought first of what others needed. And he taught his disciples to follow his example.

When we know Jesus, we want to put the needs of others ahead of our wants—as Abraham did. This is the JOY of living:

> Jesus first
> Others next
> Yourself last.

It might keep us out of some troubles. And when you get right down to it, it's the only way to real joy and happiness in this life.

Bible reading: Genesis 13:8-13

How did Lot get to choose the best land for himself? Why did this turn out to be bad for him? Why is it a good idea to think first of others?

Help us not to let our selfishness lead us into danger or wrong doing, Father. Amen.

Something to do:

Plan how you can give someone first choice before tomorrow.

RESCUED

Some people look at the trouble in the world and are discouraged. Others see the same troubles but are full of hope. What makes the difference?

The Israelites finally were able to leave Egypt. You can almost hear them breathe sighs of relief. Free at last!

Then a rumor swept through their camp: The Egyptians were coming after them! Imagine what a scare that must have given the people. How their hearts sank when they saw the clouds of dust from the chariots and soldiers of Pharaoh's army.

Now they were in a worse spot than before. They would be punished, possibly killed, for running away. And there was no way to escape, for they were right next to a large body of water.

Life often seems to be like that. We get out of one trouble and a worse one catches up to us. Anyone who has had such an experience doesn't need to be told to pray "deliver us from evil."

Some who don't believe that God delivers from evil give up when they are in trouble. The Israelites were afraid and ready to give up. They didn't stop to think of how much God had done for them.

But God can change the darkest picture. He rescued the Israelites from the Egyptian army. He led the Israelites across the sea, then let the water roll back to stop the army that was chasing them.

God does not say that trouble will never come to his people. But he does promise to be with us and to help us in our troubles. On the basis of his promise, we can pray "deliver us from evil" and be sure that God will answer.

Bible reading:
Exodus 14:10, 13-18

What evil had the Israelites escaped? What greater evil was now catching up with them? What has God promised us about the evils of this world?

Deliver us from evil of every kind, God. Thank you for your promise to be with us. Amen.

Something to do:

Find a story in your newspaper about someone who was helped out of trouble.

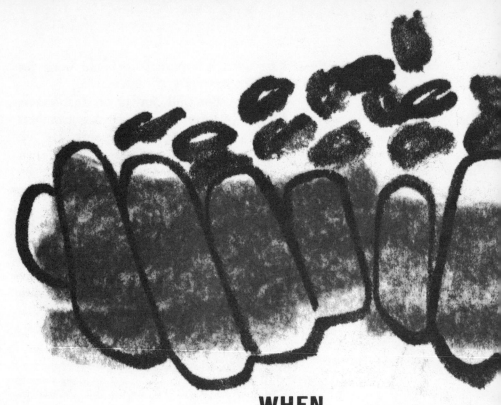

WHEN
TO SAY "WHEN"

Is it possible to ask God for too much?

When your friend pours peanuts into your hand, he may tell you, "Say when." He wants you to let him know when you have as much as you want.

Should we ever "say when" to God?

When we think about all the things we might ask God for, we may wonder, "Isn't it selfish to ask for so many things?"

98

It could be. If we ask for things we don't need; if we ask for things to get out of working for them; if we ask for something that might be harmful to us or to other people —God knows that it would not be right to give what we ask. It would be wrong too if in our prayers we asked only for things for ourselves and never thought about other people and what they need.

Yet ordinarily God doesn't want us to "say when." He wants us to keep on asking. One reason is that it is important for us to know that we can't do everything by ourselves. We all depend, in many ways, on help we get from others. If we don't understand that, our lives will be unhappy.

Most of all we need God's help, especially to live the kind of lives he wants. So we ask his help, because we know we can't do it all ourselves.

God also wants us to ask for his help because he likes to do things for people. Often it seems that he does not do what he would like to do for us until we see that we need something and ask for it.

God has even commanded us to ask for things. To encourage us to pray more, he promises many times that he will answer. We show by our prayers that we recognize his power and appreciate what he does.

Bible reading: John 16:23—24

When might it be wrong for us to ask for something? Why does God want us to ask him for things?

Keep us from being selfish in our prayers, Lord, but help us come to you in prayer for whatever we need. Amen.

A verse to remember:

"Ask and you will receive, that your joy may be full" (John 16:24).

NOT EVEN 10

Which people should we especially pray for?

God decided that he would tell Abraham the bad news about what was going to happen. Because there was so much evil in Sodom and Gomorrah, he was going to destroy those cities. Abraham knew that his nephew Lot lived in Sodom and he wanted to try to save him.

So he began to ask God to spare the city. "You wouldn't want to destroy good people who might live in the city, even if many are evil, would you?" he asked God. "If there are 50 good people in the city, will you still destroy it?"

And the Lord said, "If I find 50 righteous in the city, I'll spare the whole city."

Abraham was pleased. But as he thought about it he began to worry again. "I don't really have any right to ask this," he went on,

"but what if there are only 45 righteous people?"

The Lord answered, "I won't destroy the city if I find 45 righteous people."

Abraham tried again: "What if there are only 40?" And the an-

10 righteous people there. And God had agreed to Abraham's request.

As it happened, God didn't find 10 righteous people in that whole city, and so he destroyed it. Had Abraham's prayers been for nothing? No, because God sent angels to make sure that Lot was out of the city before it was destroyed. They almost had to carry him out to make him leave, but he was saved. It was for Lot and his family that Abraham had prayed.

God is pleased when we keep asking him for something in prayer, especially when we are asking for someone else. Often our prayers bring some good into the life of another person.

Bible reading: Genesis 18:22-23

Why was Abraham disturbed by what God told him? What did he do about it? What good did Abraham's prayers do?

Thank you, Father, for your willingness to listen to our prayers. We ask your special blessing for the people we now name. Amen.

swer was the same: "I still won't destroy the city."

"Don't get angry with me," said Abraham, "but suppose there are only 30?" Abraham kept on asking until finally he had asked God to spare the city if there were only

Something to do:

Think of people who need your prayers, and name them in a prayer of your own.

101

A CRIPPLED FRIEND

Do you know anyone who is crippled or handicapped? How do children act toward him?

People who are crippled, or who can't talk or walk as well as others, or who have something else wrong with them so they can't do everything other **people can,** have to make extra efforts just to keep up. Sometimes they have an even harder time because of the way people treat them.

Children often laugh at someone who has trouble speaking, or who can't run fast, or in some other way is different from most of us. They may even give him a nickname, like "Fatty," that makes fun of him and calls attention to something he can't help.

Older people may take advantage of a weaker person or push a crippled person out of their way. They may act as though someone isn't very smart, simply because he can't hear well or is blind. They may refuse to give him a job or a chance to do anything for himself. They may try to avoid such people, acting as though they didn't exist.

King David once learned about a crippled man named Mephibo-sheth. He was a grandson of King Saul, who had given David so much trouble and tried to keep him from becoming king. It would have been easy for David to mistreat Mephibosheth; that's what he expected. The best he could hope was for David to pay no attention to him.

But Mephibosheth was also the son of Jonathan, David's friend,

who was now dead. Thinking of his friendship for Jonathan, David decided to do something special for his crippled son. He gave Mephibosheth a place to live, and found people to work for him and care for him. And he invited Mephibosheth to eat at his palace.

When Jesus lived on earth he looked especially for those who were lame or blind or different or in need of help. He helped them and healed many. We can help blind and sick and poor people today, just as Jesus would.

Bible reading: 2 Samuel 9:1-7

Why do people mistreat cripples? What did David do for crippled Mephibosheth?

Forgive us, Lord, if we have done wrong to someone, especially someone who is handicapped. Help us to be friends especially to those who need friends most. Amen.

Something to do:

Think of someone who is crippled and plan to help him.

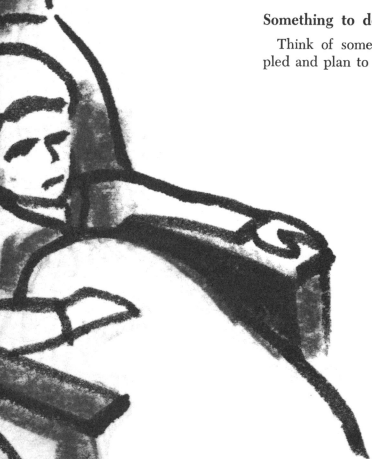

BLIND

Have you ever stopped to think what it must be like to be blind? To get some idea of what it's like walk around blindfolded for awhile, or with your eyes closed, but be sure to have someone else around so you don't bump into something.

Bartimaeus knew that it was no fun to be blind; he had been blind for a long time. How he wished he could see! Because he couldn't work at the jobs other people did, he tried to get enough money to live by begging from people who walked along the road out of the city of Jericho.

One day Bartimaeus heard that Jesus was walking down the road toward him. We don't know how he had learned about Jesus, or why he thought Jesus could help him see. He may have heard that Jesus liked to help everyone. He may have heard that Jesus healed blind people. Or maybe he knew that the Old Testament prophets told about the Savior who was to come, and that he would heal blind people and do many other wonderful things.

When Jesus came near him, Bartimaeus began to shout, "Jesus, have mercy on me." People standing around tried to keep him quiet. They thought a blind man was not important enough to bother Jesus.

But Bartimaeus knew how much it would mean for him to be able to see, and he was sure Jesus could help him. So he shouted even louder, "Jesus, have mercy on me."

Jesus heard him and stopped to talk with him. He always had time for those who needed help. He asked, "What do you want me to do for you?"

Bartimaeus said, "Master, let me receive my sight."

Jesus answered, "Your faith has made you well." And from that time on, Bartimaeus could see.

Bible reading: Mark 10:46-52

How did Jesus help Bartimaeus? How would Jesus want us to act toward blind people today?

Thank you, God, for the gift of sight. Show us how we can share the blessings we have with those who have less. Amen.

Something to do:

Think of someone you know who is blind and plan to help him in some way.

THEY LAUGHED
AT JESUS

Have you ever been laughed at?
It doesn't feel very good when
someone makes fun of us. Sometimes we forget that and begin to
tease the new boy who moves
into the neighborhood, or snicker
at the girl who doesn't have the
same kind of clothes as her class-
mates, or make fun of anybody
who is different from us in some
way.

If you've ever been laughed at,
maybe it will help to know that
people laughed at Jesus too.

Once a man came to Jesus and asked him to come home with him and heal his sick daughter. Before they came to the house, someone met them on the road and said they needn't bother Jesus about coming any more, for the girl had died. But Jesus told the father to keep believing in him and they went on.

When they reached the house they found it full of people crying and making noise. Jesus said to them, "Why are you making such a fuss? The girl is only sleeping."

The people laughed at Jesus. They knew the girl was dead, and they didn't think Jesus could do anything about it.

But Jesus paid no attention to them. He went ahead with his plans. He took the girl by the hand and said to her, "Little girl, get up." And she did. She got out of bed and walked around. She was well again. You can be sure those people didn't laugh at Jesus again.

When we're laughed at, we can learn from Jesus just to go ahead and do what we know is right. And he'll help to bring something good out of it.

Bible reading: Mark 5:35-43

Why did some people laugh at Jesus? What did he do about it? What should we do if someone makes fun of us—or of others?

When we think we're being mistreated, Jesus, help us to keep going and do what is right. Make us strong and keep us faithful to you. Amen.

Something to do:

Try to gather a bouquet of flowers and set them where you can see them for your next devotion.

107

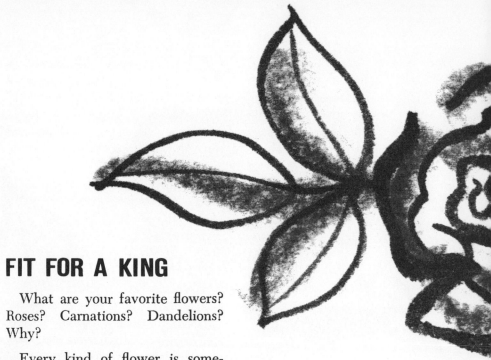

FIT FOR A KING

What are your favorite flowers? Roses? Carnations? Dandelions? Why?

Every kind of flower is somebody's favorite. Flowers are enjoyed by everyone. They add a happy touch of color to our world. Flowers are especially appreciated by those who are ill or by people celebrating a birthday or a wedding anniversary. Artists enjoy painting pictures of flowers.

Jesus must have liked flowers too. He asked his followers to notice them. "Look at them," he said. "How beautiful they are! Even King Solomon, with all his money, couldn't be clothed more beautifully than flowers."

The words of Jesus are true today. Money can't buy the beauty of the smallest flower; nobody can make anything quite as pretty.

Then Jesus asked a question: "If God provides such beauty for flowers which grow wild in the field and last only a day, won't he be sure to take even **better care** of you—his people?" The answer is that God will take much better care of us than of flowers. We are worth much more to him.

Jesus went on to say that our Father in heaven knows all the things we need in life and will see to it that we get them.

So flowers can cheer us up in at least two ways. We can enjoy their color and beauty and scent. And

they remind us that our heavenly Father cares for us.

Bible reading: Matthew 6:28-33

With whom did Jesus compare flowers? Which did he say was more glorious? What can we learn from flowers?

Thank you, Father, for the beauty of flowers, and for your loving care. Amen.

A verse to remember:

"Your heavenly Father knows that you need all these things" (Matthew 6:32).

THEY HADN'T CAUGHT A THING

If you like to go fishing, think of the time you caught the most fish. Have you ever gone fishing without catching a single one?

Several of Jesus' disciples made their living by catching and selling fish. Sometimes they filled their large nets. Other times they came back from the sea with empty nets.

Once so many people crowded around Jesus that he had to get into a boat. He talked to the people on the shore. Then he told the disciples to row out into deeper water and throw out their nets to catch some fish. Peter answered, "We worked all night and didn't catch a thing." But because he had learned that Jesus always had a reason for what he told them, he added, "But if you say so, we will try again." He was in for a surprise!

This time they caught so many fish that their nets began to break. When Peter saw this, he realized Jesus had done a miracle, and he said a strange thing. "Depart from me," he told Jesus, "for I am a sinful man." He understood that Jesus

must have the power of God to be able to do such a miracle. And he knew that God is holy, but that he was just a sinful man. He didn't think he was good enough or important enough to be near God.

Jesus told him not to be afraid to be near him. Peter did not need to fear and we don't need to be afraid either. God uses his power to help us, not to make us afraid. And Jesus added, "From now on you will catch men."

We can be fishers of men, too. Even if we aren't the best fishermen, we can be fishers of men by telling others about Jesus and what he does for us. We don't have to be experts. Jesus will bring results, just as in the miracle of the fishes.

Bible reading: Luke 5:3-11

Why didn't Peter want to go fishing again? Why did he tell Jesus, "Depart from me"? How can we be fishers of men?

We thank you, Lord, that you use your power to help us. Help us to be fishers of men for you. Amen.

Something to do:

Think of someone you can invite to church or Sunday school with you next Sunday.

111

PARENTS AND A PROMISE

Only one of the Ten Commandments includes a promise. Do you know which one it is?

God promised that certain people would live a long time, and that things would go well for them. This will happen, he said, to those who honor their father and mother. It would be hard to measure how much children honor their parents. Sometimes those who seem to be honoring their parents most really don't honor them in their thoughts or in what they do at home. Others who say very little about it may be honoring their parents the most.

What does it mean to honor your parents? It means to respect them; to listen to their advice; to obey them. It means to be thankful for all that parents do. And since parents aren't perfect, it means to forgive them when they do wrong. Above all, it means to love parents —to return the love they give.

What if parents aren't good? Sometimes this happens. Then we should do what we know is right

before God rather than do something wrong. This isn't likely to happen often.

Almost all parents do the best they can for their children. They have been given a job from God— to train their children. We can respect them for the responsibility they have, and we can be courteous to them as we are to all people, especially those who are older.

The Bible often tells children to obey their parents. But it speaks to parents too. When both parents and children honor the Lord by doing what he says, all will be well for both of them. We can love one another as parents and children when we live in the sureness of God's love for us.

Bible reading: Ephesians 6:1-4

Why should children obey parents? What can a child do if he thinks his parents aren't doing what God wants? What if parents think children aren't doing what God wants?

Father, thank you for parents. Help all parents do what you want. Help all children to honor their parents in the Lord. Amen.

A verse to remember:

"Children, obey your parents in the Lord, for this is right" (Ephesians 6:1).

GLAD TO GO

Do you like to go to church? Why?

Some people like to go to church. King David was one of them. He said, "I was glad when they said to me, 'Let us go to the house of the Lord.'"

Others may attend church at times, but they aren't happy about it. They do their best to think up an excuse for not going. They go only because someone, perhaps their mother, makes them go—or because they hope people will think more highly of them—or because they think they are doing God a favor by going, and they expect he'll pay them back later.

Others never even think about whether they like to go to church. They may attend out of habit, or because others do. Some ask themselves every Sunday, "Shall I go to church today?" And whether they go or not depends on how they feel, or what else they can think of doing.

How can we learn to like going to church?

Well, why do you like to go to anyone's house? Usually your reasons are connected with the person or persons you'll be with in the other house. You love this person and enjoy his company. You feel you gain something by being with him.

If we think of God as a friend, we will surely like to go to his house. If we don't know him very well or are afraid of him, we may want to stay away.

In addition, if we know some of the good things God has done for us we want to go to his house. We want to thank him, and to let others know how much we think of him. We'll also go because we know that we receive something more from him every time. We may go too because we enjoy being with his family—the other people who believe in God.

Even if we think some things are not exactly as they should be—if the service is too long, or if the words are hard to understand—when we love God we are still glad to go to his house.

Bible reading: Psalm 122:1

Why do some people not like to go to church? What reasons can you think of why you like to go? What could we do to make church going more enjoyable?

Thank you, God, that we have the chance to gather in your house to learn more of your love for us. Help us make use of these opportunities with joy. Amen.

Something to do:

Try to find the theme for next Sunday's service. Read the Bible passages and sing one of the hymns that may be used.

115

THREE QUESTIONS

Has something ever happened on a picnic that you will never forget?

The disciples never forgot a "picnic" that took place some time after Jesus rose from death. They had gone fishing. Since they had fished for a living all their lives it was natural for them to go out in a boat when they didn't know what else to do. They didn't seem to be quite sure what Jesus wanted them to be doing now.

They fished all night long, but caught nothing. As the sun was coming up they saw a man standing on the shore of the lake. He asked them if they had caught anything. When they said "No," he told them to put their net down on the right side of the boat. They did as he said, and this time they had so many fish they couldn't pull the net out of the water.

Then they knew that the person on the shore was Jesus. By the time they got to shore, dragging their net full of fish, he had built a camp-

fire and was cooking breakfast for them.

After they had eaten, Jesus asked Peter, "Do you love me?"

Peter remembered the time he had said he didn't even know Jesus, much less love him. He must have remembered too how he had boasted that he would never leave Jesus, even if others did.

This time he did not brag. He just said quietly, "You know that I love you."

Three times Jesus asked him the question. When Peter answered that he did love Jesus, Jesus told him to feed or care for his sheep. By this he meant that Peter was to teach people about God's love for them.

Peter is not the only one who has been asked whether he loves Jesus. It happens to all of us. It may not be in those exact words; the question may not even be in words. Instead, we may have a chance to answer the question by the way we act. Whether or not we do what Jesus asked Peter to do, that is to help the people Jesus loves, shows how much we love him.

Bible reading: John 21:4-17

What did Jesus ask Peter? What did Jesus tell him to do? How do we show our love for Jesus?

Forgive us for acting at times as though we don't love you, Jesus. We do love you. Help us to show love in our lives. Amen.

Something to do:

Think of at least one thing to do tomorrow that will show your love for Jesus.

SCHOOL'S OPEN

What do you have to look forward to in school next year? What will be different?

The first day of school is always an exciting day in any family. There are many things to get ready: clothes, pencils, paper, and other things needed for class work. We may have to change our schedules and start getting up earlier to catch a bus or walk to school on time. There may be lunches to prepare. We may wonder what the new teacher or the new subjects will be like. We look forward to being with our friends again. Some children are happy when school begins again. Others wish vacation could last forever.

In all the bustle of getting ready, we may not even think about the reasons for going to school. We just know it's something everyone has to do. It's good sometimes for families to talk about why we go to school, and what we hope to get out of it. This might help us enjoy school more.

We go to school to learn, of course, and there are many important things to learn in school. But the Bible says that the most impor-

tant thing to learn is the fear and love of God. The writer of Proverbs said several times, to be sure we wouldn't miss it, "The fear of the Lord is the beginning of knowledge."

If we don't know about God and his love for us, all the learning we do in schools will still leave out the one thing that can make the greatest difference in our lives. If we begin our education by having faith in God, what we learn in school will mean more to us, as we see how we can use our learning to do what God wants us to do.

118

Bible reading: Proverbs 1:7-9

What does the Bible say is the first thing we should learn? How can believing in God make a difference in what we learn in school?

We thank you for the opportunities we have to attend school, Father. Help the teachers to do their jobs well. Help all students to learn what is most important for them. Amen.

A verse to remember:

"The fear of the Lord is the beginning of knowledge" (Proverbs 1:7).

THE BEST
PLACE TO LEARN

When do you learn most about God and what he wants you to do?

Moses didn't have a church building with classrooms. Nor did he teach any Sunday school classes. But he knew how people learn about God. He knew that everybody is learning about God and how to act toward him all the time —and everywhere.

120

What we learn isn't always correct; sometimes we learn or teach the wrong things. As we see what other people do and hear what they say, whether it's good or bad, we begin to copy them. Others are watching us too and may learn from what we are doing, even if we have never thought of ourselves as teachers. Most of what we learn about our religion is taught away from the church building—most often in the home.

Moses knew this. He told the Israelites how important it was to learn the truth about God, and he urged parents to teach God's word to their children. This should be done, he said, not just once or twice, or on the Sabbath, or when you're in a class, but when you're walking along a street, or when you lie down, or when you get up.

In other words, we should be teaching and learning about God all the time. Some of the Israelites wound leather straps around their hands and head to remind them to think about God. Even today many Jews put a little metal plate called a *mezuzah* on their doors as a reminder.

It would be good for us to have such reminders too. For if it is as important to love God and learn about him as the church says and as Christians believe, we ought to have that in our mind all the time. It's something to think about— when you get up, when you go to bed, when you are walking around, when you're talking with others.

Bible reading: Deuteronomy 6:4-9

When were the Israelites told to think about God? When should we think about God? What can help us to do this?

Help us, Lord, to think of you often as we go about our daily work. Amen.

Something to do:

Make something to display somewhere in your home to remind you of God's love.

121

A CHANCE TO ASK QUESTIONS

Who taught you most about God? Who do you think taught Jesus?

Jesus liked to ask questions. He knew that that is the way to learn. As he was growing up, there were many things for him to learn, just as for all of us. Although Jesus didn't go to a school like ours, many people taught him what he needed to know. Some of those teachers were the priests in the temple.

Since the temple was in Jerusalem, far from Jesus' home in Nazareth, his family didn't get there very often. But they went there for a special celebration at least once a year. When Jesus was 12 years old he went with them.

When he was at the temple, Jesus got so interested in talking with the priests that he forgot what time it was or where his parents were. Have you ever been that interested in something?

When the celebration was over, his parents started out on their trip back home. There were so many people on the road with them that they didn't realize Jesus wasn't along. They thought he was with some of the other boys from their neighborhood, or with relatives.

Later they began to wonder where he was. They asked if anyone had seen Jesus. No one had. It soon became clear that he wasn't anywhere among the people on the road. His worried parents hurried back to Jerusalem to look for him. After searching a long time, they finally found Jesus in the temple—where they had all been earlier in the week.

He wasn't lost; he was just making use of the chance to learn about God by asking questions. The priests were pleased to find a boy so interested in learning about God, just as a pastor today is happy to have a child—or a grown-up—ask questions.

Bible reading: Luke 2:41-52

Why didn't Mary and Joseph go to the temple often? What did Jesus do there? Of whom can we ask questions to learn about God?

Lord, we thank you for those who have taught us about you. Help us to teach someone else. Amen.

Something to do:

Think of some questions you would like your pastor to answer, then go and ask him.

123

INDEX OF BIBLICAL REFERENCES